MANCHESTER
MURDERS AND
MISDEMEANOURS

ADRIAN & DAWN L. BRIDGE

AMBERLEY

It is with true empathy that we dedicate this book to the memory of the victims of the crimes included within these pages, and their families, and also to all those who dedicate their lives to making our communities safer places to live.

First published 2023

Amberley Publishing
The Hill, Stroud
Gloucestershire, GL5 4EP

www.amberley-books.com

British Library Cataloguing in Publication Data.
A catalogue record for this book is available from the British Library.

ISBN 978 1 3981 1455 5 (paperback)
ISBN 978 1 3981 1456 2 (ebook)

Typesetting by Hurix Digital, India.
Printed in Great Britain.

CONTENTS

INTRODUCTION

The period between 1850 and 1950 was a time of incredible change in Manchester, and in the world as a whole. In 1850, Manchester was the prototype of a new kind of industrialised city. It was the centre of the Lancashire cotton industry, with hundreds of cotton mills churning out goods which were sold around the world. The city was, however, much more than just 'Cottonopolis'. It was a centre of banking, economic and political thought, science, and innovation in general. Manchester continued to expand its geographical boundaries throughout the period, during times of both economic boom and bust. To the west, the great neighbouring 'twin city' of Salford acquired its own borough charter in 1844, which restricted Manchester's expansion in this area. Nevertheless, police and criminals moved freely between Salford borough and Manchester city, so the following account will include crimes and misdemeanours committed in both areas. To the south, however, nearby townships were incorporated within the city of Manchester on a regular basis, including Rusholme in 1885, Withington in 1904, and Northenden in 1931. By 1950, an urban ribbon connected Manchester with many Lancashire and Cheshire towns such as Oldham, Bury, Rochdale and Stockport, forming the vast north-west conurbation known in more modern times as Greater Manchester. The unique, unplanned industrial colossus of Manchester which arose in the 1850s attracted crime and criminality of all kinds.

Manchester from Kersal Moor, by William Wyld (1852).

Many crimes were committed in Manchester's poorest, most densely populated areas (the so-called 'rookeries') such as Deansgate, and Angel Meadow in the north-east of the city. No areas, though, were exempted entirely from the impact of lawlessness. As will be seen in the following pages, crimes could be committed in Manchester and Salford at any time of day or night, and at any location, from exclusive hotels and mansions to shops, railway stations and dark street corners. Readers might well be aware of some of the people and crimes recounted during this exploration of the seamier side of Manchester life between 1850 and 1950. The authors have, however, delved through a hundred years of newspaper accounts, court reports and other original sources in an endeavour to find much that is new and perhaps surprising on the subject of 'Manchester Murders and Misdemeanours'. We hope that you find our account an enjoyable and informative one.

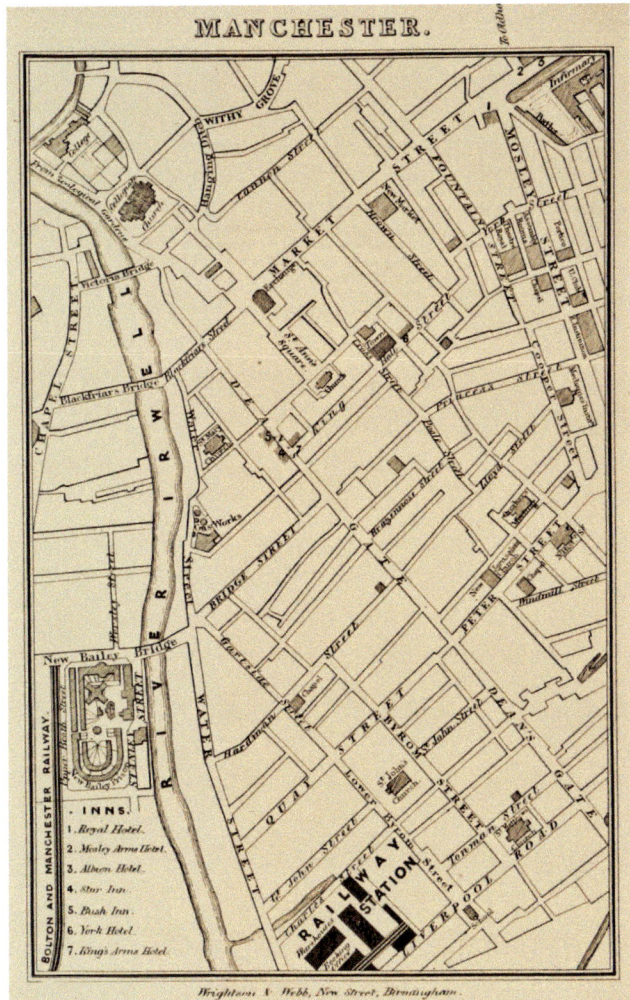

1839 map of Manchester. (© British Library)

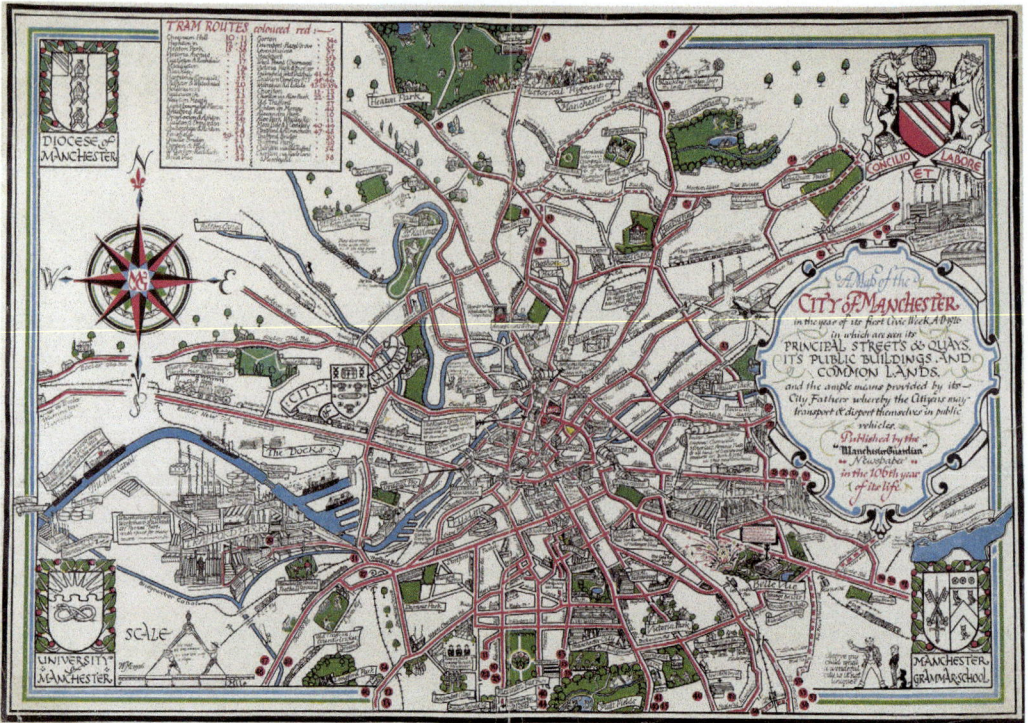

Map of Manchester dated 2 October 1926, signed by WM.

THE MANCHESTER ASSIZES AND POLICE COURTS

The courts of assize (or assizes) have a long history going back to at least 1293, when groups of judges first began travelling around four circuits or areas of England and Wales, presiding over periodic courts and dispensing justice. By 1378 there were six such circuits, and by 1876 this figure had grown to seven. Historically, Manchester and Lancashire formed part of the Northern Circuit, where periodic assize courts would take place which exercised jurisdiction over both civil and criminal matters. In the pre-railway age, Lancaster was the only location in the entire county where assize courts took place. However, as the Industrial Revolution took off, and population figures shot up in the industrialised centres of the north-west, new assize courts were created in Liverpool and then Manchester. The new assizes court constructed in Manchester between 1859 and 1864 reflected the extreme confidence and opulence of the city in the mid-nineteenth century. The building itself, situated on Great Ducie Street in Strangeways, was designed in the Venetian Gothic style by the renowned Victorian architect Alfred Waterhouse, and the nearby Strangeways prison was also included within the overall judicial building scheme. Between 1864 and 1877, the imposing building dominated the Manchester skyline as the city's tallest building, but the structure was damaged severely in the German aerial blitz of 1940–41. Almost everything of note in this impressive edifice was destroyed by German bombs, other than the judges' lodgings and the Great Ducie Street façade. These remaining remnants of the former assizes court were, perhaps not surprisingly, demolished in 1957, a year after the assizes court system was finally brought to an end in both Manchester and Liverpool. Manchester Assizes Court remains one of the great lost buildings of the city of Manchester, and within its confines some of the greatest and most complex cases in English legal history were conducted. The city's status as an assize town meant that some trials took place for crimes that had little or nothing to do with Manchester. In 1935, for instance, the Indian-born doctor Buck Ruxton was arrested for the murder of his common law wife, Isabella, and the family's maid, Jane Rogerson, in Lancaster. The city of Lancaster was some 70 miles from Manchester, but the 'savage surgeon', as Ruxton was sometimes called, still ended up being tried for his life at the Manchester Assizes in March 1936.

Left: Alfred Waterhouse.
(© Victoria Gallery &
Museum, Liverpool)

Below: Manchester Assizes
Court interior, *c.* 1890s
(unknown photographer).

Strangeways entrance. (© Peter McDermott)

Buck Ruxton's trial in Manchester proved to be one of the legal sensations of the 1930s. Teams of brilliant barristers were involved in both prosecuting and defending Ruxton during the eleven-day trial. Famous King's Councillors (KC's) such as David Maxwell Fyfe and Hartley Shawcross led the prosecution case, while Norman Birkett KC put up a spirited defence on behalf of Ruxton. The double murders proved to be grisly affairs, with both victims being dismembered after death. Ruxton then took various body parts, wrapped in newspaper, to Moffat in Dumfriesshire, where he dumped the incriminating packages in the Gardenholme Linn stream. Some pioneering forensic techniques were used by scientists at Edinburgh University, led by Professor John Glaister, to identify the human remains, and to establish the causes of death for both women. This scientific evidence proved pretty conclusively that Ruxton was the culprit, and it took the jury just one hour to find him guilty of both murders. Justice John Singleton sentenced Ruxton to death, and the so-called savage surgeon was hanged at Strangeways Prison, on 12 May 1936, by the well-known executioner Albert Pierrepoint. A day after his execution, a brief confession note was published in which Ruxton admitted murdering his wife in a fit of jealous rage (he suspected her of numerous infidelities). The unfortunate maid had witnessed Ruxton killing his wife, which explains why she also had to die.

Fortunately, gruesome murders like those committed by Buck Ruxton were very rare indeed, and there were relatively few murder trials conducted at the Manchester Assizes. In both the spring and autumn assizes of 1900, for example, no murder cases at all were tried in Manchester. In most other Manchester Assize Court sessions, however, there were usually at least one or two murder

David Maxwell Fyfe sketch, by Laura Knight, *c.* 1946.

Gardenholme Linn. (© James Towill)

cases brought before judge and jury for consideration. Of course, not all murder charges brought to the assize court ended in trial by jury. At the commencement of every Manchester Assize Court session, be it winter, spring, summer or autumn, a grand jury met (supervised by the session's judge) in order to decide whether there was enough evidence to bring an individual, or individuals, to trial for a particular offence. The grand jury system ended in Britain and Wales in 1933, though it continues in the USA to the present day. On occasions, the Manchester grand jury did drop cases brought before it, under guidance from the particular judge in charge. On the commencement of the Manchester Winter Assizes in November 1882, for instance, Mr Justice Day and the grand jury dropped murder charges against an individual who (in their opinion) was clearly insane, and therefore not responsible for his/her actions. In addition, Justice Day successfully persuaded the Manchester grand jury to throw out a charge of burglary against another individual facing trial. Manchester grand juries could also act entirely on their own initiative. When the first assize sessions opened in 1864, following the completion of Waterhouse's court buildings, the grand jury presented a petition from all the jurors asking that the national government take swift action to end the practice of public executions. The judge in charge of proceedings then promised to forward this petition to the Home Secretary. Ultimately, public executions were ended, but the procedure for ending the spectacle of public hangings proved to be far from swift. Clearly, only a small proportion of Manchester Assize Court's time was taken up with murder cases. Other crimes such as robbery, burglary and counterfeiting of coinage were judged on a far more frequent basis. The crime of 'coining' – tendering counterfeit coins in payment of goods and services – featured constantly in trials at Manchester Assizes. Forged banknotes were less of a problem, because criminals found it difficult to produce realistic looking watermarks. Passing fake silver coins was far easier, and catching the criminals who engaged in such activities was very difficult indeed. Coiners had to be either caught in the act of tendering fake coins, or at the premises where the forgery took place, in order for there to be a realistic chance of an arrest and a subsequent conviction. Once coiners were arrested and convicted, sentences handed out at Manchester Assizes were often very severe. The disastrous economic consequences of rampant coining were often cited as the reasons for such severity. In January 1884, for instance, an elderly man named Jones, together with a thirteen-year-old boy called John Wheel, pleaded guilty at Manchester Assizes to being in possession of 247 counterfeit coins 'with intent to utter them', which was the rather arcane phrase used to describe coiners who were just about to buy goods and services with their fake money. Despite his age, the judge sentenced Jones to five years in prison. The young boy, who might or might not have been Jones' son, and who declined to give an account of himself during the trial, was sentenced to one month in prison, with hard labour, followed by detention in a reformatory for a further four years.

MANCHESTER'S POLICE COURTS

Manchester's city police courts, county police courts (which covered areas away from the city centre such as Withington, Rusholme and Eccles) and Salford's police court dealt with a vast array of crimes and misdemeanours. All classes and types of people passed through police court docks, from those accused of murder, assault and other serious offences, down to the beggars, prostitutes, pickpockets, and other petty thieves who thronged the streets of the city. In May 1897, the *Manchester Evening News* published Manchester city police court's full accounts for the financial year ending on 31 March, and analysis of the court's sources of income says much about what crimes and misdemeanours were most common in the city. The published accounts also give a good indication of what was happening in Salford and the outlying areas of the Manchester conurbation, because the Salford police court, and the Manchester county police court, dealt with the same problems and issues as the Manchester city police court. Fines levied for being drunk and disorderly, and for assault, were by far the most common financial penalties imposed by the city police court in the year 1896–97 (and the same was true for many years both before and after the 1897 publication of police court accounts). Excessive drinking affected all classes of people in Manchester, and in 1874 *The Graphic* newspaper reported that over 10,000 cases of drunkenness were heard before Manchester police court magistrates every year. Repeat offenders faced obvious health dangers, as was illustrated by the sad case of the often inebriated Amy Chatterton, who dropped dead in the city police court dock, in August 1892, as she faced charges of being drunk and disorderly. Young children were also prosecuted for drunkenness: In February 1866, an unnamed eleven-year-old girl was given a warning, and then discharged, after appearing before Mr Robinson Fowler at the Manchester city police court, accused of being drunk and disorderly. The girl, somewhat alarmingly, claimed that her drinks had been 'spiked' with raw spirits by an accompanying adult. Perhaps surprisingly, the city police court also spent much time cracking down on incidents of animal cruelty. During the 1896–97 financial year, £269 was levied in fines on those who were adjudged to be guilty of animal cruelty in some way. The Manchester county and Salford police courts gave the same priority to animal related cases, and sometimes handed out stiff penalties to those found to be contravening the relevant laws. In August 1876, for instance, at Salford police court, Bernard Sherry was sentenced to three months in prison, with hard labour, for the offence of plucking a fowl while it was still alive. Two years earlier, in April 1874, the county police court sentenced an offender named Herbert Stratham (an Eccles carter) to three months hard labour in prison for stealing two terrier dogs. On 20 June 1903 the same court had no difficulty in finding an unnamed defendant guilty of shooting dead a homing pigeon flying between Crewe and Preston. The offender had to pay fines totalling more than £6 – no mean sum at the time, and roughly equivalent to well over £700 in 2022.

Manchester Police Court, Minshull Street. (© KJP1)

Above: Earliest known image of Salford Town Hall, *c.* 1856 (unknown photographer).

Below: Salford Town Hall. (© Barrie Price)

THE GARIBALDI OF DETECTIVES

Jerome Caminada was born in 1844 in Deansgate, which at the time was considered to be a notorious sinkhole of criminality, full of brothels and down-at-heel alehouses. Jerome's father was an Italian, his mother was Irish, and young Jerome was educated at the catholic St Mary's school, where he proved to be a rather average scholar. After leaving school he worked for a number of years at the Sharpe & Stewart engineering works, and then at Mather & Platt. In 1868, however, Jerome Caminada found his true vocation in life when he joined A Division of the Manchester City Police force, under Superintendent Gee. During the subsequent thirty-one years, Caminada's police career became the stuff of legend. In 1871, he was promoted to sergeant and transferred to Manchester's fledgling detective section. In 1882 he became an inspector, and in 1884 he was made a chief inspector. Finally, in 1897, he became the superintendent of the entire Manchester detective division. During the course of his police career, Caminada was responsible for apprehending over 1,250 offenders. The people he arrested also generated £9,300 in fines for the coffers of the Manchester City, County, and Salford police courts. It was in every way a stellar career in law enforcement, and one that was recognised at the time by judges, politicians and newspapers across Britain. By the end of the 1880s, Caminada was one of the most famous policemen in Britain, and his praises were sung publicly by eighteen different High Court judges. Justice Edward Abbott Parry once referred to Caminada as being the 'Garibaldi of detectives,' which was a very high honour indeed for a Victorian judge to bestow on any individual. Giuseppe Garibaldi was one of

Jerome Caminada in 1890 (unknown photographer).

the crucial architects of the Italian Risorgimento – the unification of Italy into one distinct, independent political entity. Obviously, Caminada was half Italian. The analogy does, however, go much deeper than this. For many Victorians, Garibaldi was the perfect model of a man; someone who combined great idealism with passion and enormous vigour. To say that Caminada was the 'Garibaldi of detectives' therefore says much about the high esteem and veneration in which the Manchester detective was held not just by Parry, but by great swathes of the more general British population.

Justice Edward Parry (later Sir Edward) was a judge at the Manchester County Court for many years, and knew Jerome Caminada quite well. During summer 1898, both men were at the centre of one of Manchester's most unusual criminal cases – one which involved the attempted murder of Justice Parry during an actual session of the Manchester County Court, held in Quay Street, on 25 July. On the morning of the 25th, Parry delivered a judgement on a civil case involving an authorised bailiff of the County Court called William Taylor. The Singer Machine Company complained that Taylor had exceeded his authority by seizing goods rented by the company to individuals who later turned out to be in debt. Justice Parry found in favour of the company, and also acted in response to more general complaints that Taylor had charged too much for his services as a bailiff. William Taylor's rights as a bailiff were removed with immediate

Giuseppe Garibaldi, *c.* 1861.
(© Library of Congress)

effect. Taylor was present in the courtroom when the decision was made, which ruined his livelihood, and he responded immediately by charging towards Parry and shooting him at close quarters with an old revolver. Edward Parry was shot three times, with bullets lodging in his neck and cheek. Not surprisingly, mayhem ensued in the court. Parry was taken away for emergency treatment, and William Taylor was restrained by court officials and others present at the scene.

Detective Superintendent Caminada arrived quickly at the scene, and was soon questioning Taylor about the incident. Both Caminada and Taylor then travelled back to detective headquarters at Manchester Town Hall, where the ex-bailiff was formally charged with attempted murder, and then lodged in one of the Town Hall police cells. William Taylor certainly seemed to regret his actions, and mentioned in his interviews with Caminada (much to the delight of the Victorian press) that his murderous assault on Judge Parry had been 'done by satanic influence'. In reality, Taylor faced acute financial problems at the time, which were certainly exacerbated by the loss of his bailiff's accreditation, and it was this that led to his wild attack on Parry in the Manchester County Courtroom. When the case came to trial at the Manchester Assizes, on 16 September 1898, the result was never really in much doubt. It took the jury less than fifteen minutes to find Taylor guilty of attempted murder, though the jury

Manchester County Court, Quay Street. (© KJP1)

foreman asked the trial judge (Justice Philimore) to be merciful in his sentencing because of Taylor's age – he was fifty-six – and because of his previous good character. Philimore, however, proved to be somewhat less than forgiving, and sentenced William Taylor to twenty years in prison. Judge Parry subsequently made a speedy recovery from his gunshot wounds, and was back at work in the Manchester County Court by the end of November 1898. Solving the attempted murder of Judge Parry required no real detective work on the part of Jerome Caminada – the offender was, after all, caught red-handed at the scene of the crime. Most of the investigations conducted by this 'Garibaldi of detectives' were far more complex, and required far more thought and attention than the Parry case. Probably the most famous crime investigated, and solved, by Caminada was the so-called Hansom cab murder of 1889. On 26 February 1889, John Fletcher, a prominent retired paper manufacturer, and a Lancashire county councillor, was found slumped in the back of a Hansom cab in Manchester. The door to the cab was open, and the passenger who had journeyed with Fletcher in the conveyance was nowhere to be seen. An unconscious Fletcher was taken to the Manchester Royal Infirmary (MRI) but unfortunately died en route, and Jerome Caminada was called in to investigate the puzzling death of the local businessman.

Manchester Town Hall. (© Samuel Vincent)

Above: Hansom cab with driver and passenger inside, 1884. (© Library of Congress)

Below: Manchester Royal Infirmary (MRI), *c.* 1905. (© Ardfern)

It took Caminada roughly three weeks to investigate and solve the case, in what was probably his finest moment as a Manchester detective. A coroner decided that John Fletcher had died as a result of the combined effects of alcohol and the ingestion of the sedative chloryl hydrate. Caminada began to hunt for a criminal who had killed Fletcher with chloryl and then stolen the retired businessman's watch, watch guard and money. A number of witnesses came forward to say that they had seen Fletcher get into a cab with a young man. Other witnesses also stated that they had seen a man drinking with Fletcher in the Three Arrows public house in Deansgate. Moreover, these same witnesses claimed to have seen the unnamed man slip a phial of some unidentifiable liquid into Fletcher's drinks at the Three Arrows. A crucial development in the case came when Caminada linked the use of chloryl hydrate to the Victorian prize fighting circuit. The chemical was used, illegally, to subdue and sedate opponents in the ring, and Caminada began to look for a killer with boxing connections. Very quickly, young Charles Parton, aged twenty-one, became the main focus of police investigations. Parton was a prize fighter who had two boxing brothers and a father who was also a retired prize fighter. Under questioning from Caminada, and other policemen, Charles Parton admitted administering chloryl to John Fletcher. The young prize fighter subsequently became the first person ever to be charged with murdering someone via the administration of chloryl hydrate. It's unclear whether Parton actually intended to kill the unfortunate Fletcher, whom he'd first met when working at a local hotel. Parton had sedated and then robbed previous victims, and claimed that on this occasion he'd accidently overdone the doses of chloryl given to Fletcher. Nevertheless, he was still found guilty of wilful murder at his trial at the Manchester Assizes, and sentenced to death. His execution was scheduled to take place on 9 April 1889. However, doubts remained in some legal circles about the efficacy of the final verdict, particularly given Parton's relative youth, and the sentence of death was commuted to one of life imprisonment. Young Parton turned out to be a model prisoner, and as a result of his good behaviour, he was released from custody after serving just eleven years and nine months of his original life sentence. Victorians called this early release system 'ticket-of-leave' and it was a system which was criticised constantly by those who thought prisons, and the judiciary as a whole, were too soft in their treatment of offenders.

Ironically, Parton was again in trouble with the authorities, soon after his early release. The ex-prize fighter found himself back in prison for ten days after stealing a watch in Hull. Much later on, in 1925, the fifty-seven-year-old Parton was sentenced to three months in prison, with hard labour, for stealing a woman's purse in Southampton. As he was sentenced for this last theft, in Southampton, Parton claimed that he was a marked man, targetted by the police, and never given a fair chance in life. Clearly, he was never able to fully escape the notoriety of his 1889 crimes, and never able to live a stable, law-abiding life. The capture and conviction of Charles Parton was certainly a significant triumph for Jerome Caminada. Another of his major successes was the final tracking down and

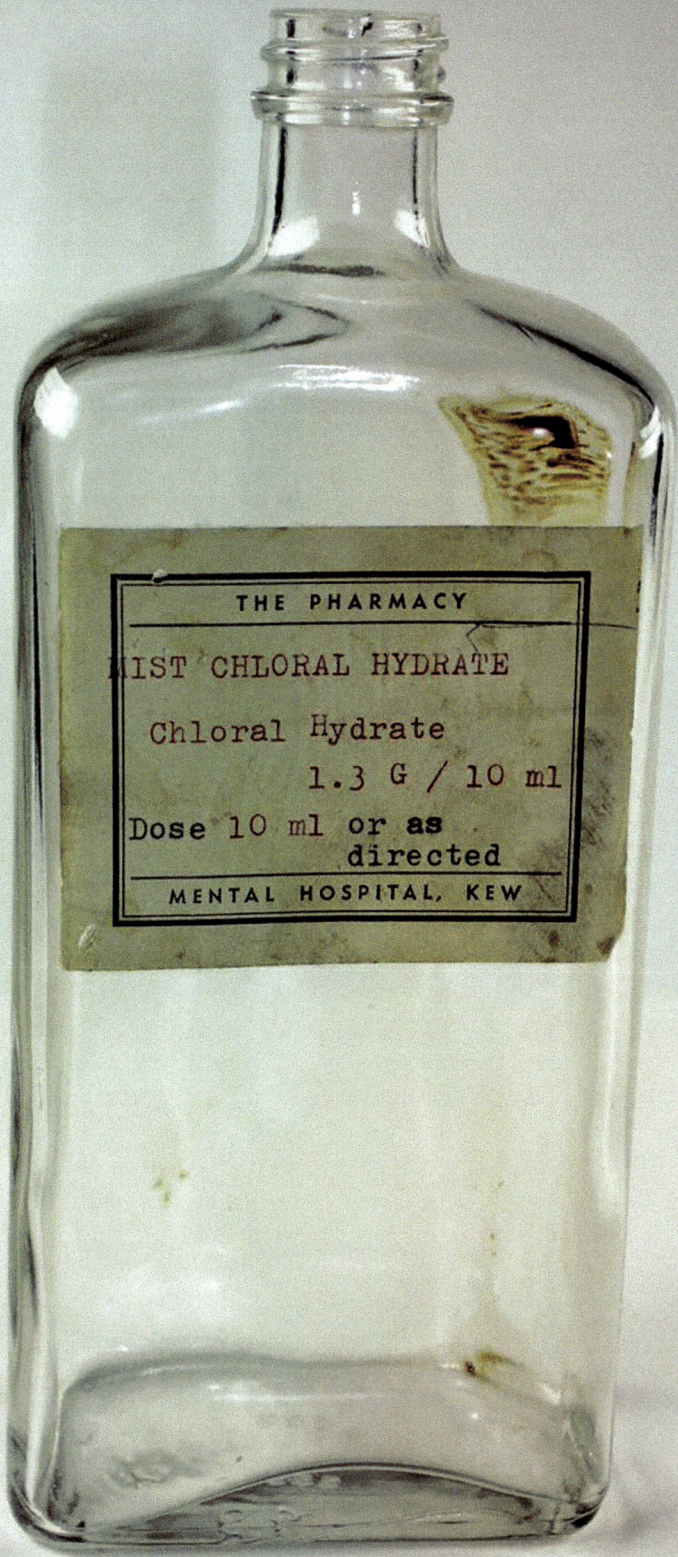

Victorian chloryl hydrate apothecary jar. (© Museums Victoria)

capture of Robert Horridge, who proved to be one of Victorian Manchester's most violent and ruthless criminals. Horridge was born in the Strangeways area in 1845, committed his first offence as a thirteen year old, and went on to become a thorn in the side of the Manchester police force for the following thirty years. Caminada arrested Horridge on two occasions during the early part of his police career, firstly for receiving stolen goods, and then in 1870 for the theft of a watch. During the 1870s and early 1880s Horridge was in and out of prison for various offences, but by summer 1887 he was again on the loose and planning further robberies in Manchester. On 30 July 1887, Horridge attempted to rob Angus Wood's shoe shop on Rochdale Road, along with a female accomplice named Elizabeth Stone. However, the noise created by Horridge and Stone during their attempted robbery attracted the attention of a policeman on patrol. PC Bannon came to investigate, and a desperate fight ensued between the policeman and Horridge, who was armed with a loaded revolver. Horridge fired once at Bannon, grazing his face with a bullet. The policeman blew his whistle in order to summon help, and PC Parkin arrived at the shoe shop within a few minutes. Horridge shot the newly arrived constable in the stomach, and then ran off into the night. Fortunately, Parkin survived his life-threatening injuries, and Elizabeth Stone was also detained at the scene of the robbery. Manchester police then began a huge manhunt for the fugitive Horridge, and Jerome Caminada and his detective team were at the forefront of this major operation. Caminada quickly tracked Horridge to Liverpool, and in a dramatic encounter in the middle of Duke Street, the Manchester detective (disguised as a labourer) was able to seize and arrest the violent shoe shop robber. Both men were armed when they met and scuffled in Duke Street. Caminada often carried a Colt Lightening revolver with him, and Horridge had a loaded revolver in his pocket. However, threats from Caminada that he would fire his Colt seem to have persuaded Horridge not to try and go for his gun. Robert Horridge's days of freedom were over, and in November 1887, at the Manchester Assizes, he was found guilty of the attempted murders of PCs Bannon and Parkin and sentenced to life imprisonment. Horridge was eventually released from custody in October 1907, after serving nearly twenty years in prison, and by 1911 he was living a quiet, rather obscure life as a peddler in Cheetham Hill.

During the course of his long police career, Jerome Caminada was thoroughly at home on the teeming streets of Manchester, mixing with its polyglot population, and keeping abreast of the latest criminal activity via the extensive use of a highly personalised network of informants, many of whom he met at St Mary's Church, on Mulberry Street, in central Manchester. Caminada was never afraid of leading from the front, and he was often the first man through the door on a number of major police raids targeting illegal gambling dens, coining operations, and other suspected criminal activities. In late 1891, for example, he led a squad of officers who raided premises being used by two major coining gangs. Some of the gang members resisted strongly, and were only arrested after a huge fight with police officers. Over 100 counterfeit coins were discovered in the possession of gang

Colt Lightening gun, 1877. (© Hmaag)

members, along with a machine for producing forged money. In a major coup for Caminada, the so-called 'king of the coiners', John Ryan, was also captured during this raid on the two coining gangs. In excess of 530 forged half-crowns and florins were found in Ryan's possession. The king of the coiners was seventy years old at the time of his arrest, and told Caminada that he'd probably die in prison once he was tried and convicted for these latest coining offences. The counterfeiter seems to have accepted his fate with considerable *sang froid*, and gave his Meershaum pipe to Caminada as a keepsake. Two years before John Ryan's arrest, Caminada, along with Manchester's Chief Constable, Malcolm Wood, led a large number of police officers in a massive raid on a Liberal Party constituency meeting being held at Hulme Town Hall. The object of the raid, on 29 January 1889, was to arrest the Irish Nationalist MP William O'Brien, who was scheduled to speak at the event. O'Brien was wanted in Dublin by the Royal Irish Constabulary, and although Caminada and Wood managed to detain O'Brien, they only did so after a massive brawl in which the Chief Constable was knocked to the floor by an O'Brien supporter. Caminada came to Wood's aid by flattening the attacker with a huge blow to the side of the head, and O'Brien was subsequently taken to Manchester Town Hall, and then escorted back to Dublin.

Probably the best known of the Caminada-led police raids was the one launched against the attendees at the famous cross-dressing ball held at Hulme Temperance Hall on 24 September 1880. Following a tip-off to the Chief Constable that 'immoral' acts between men were due to take place at the ball, Caminada and a team of police officers raided the establishment. Inside the venue, they discovered forty-seven men, twenty-two of whom were dressed as women. Virtually everyone

St Mary's Church, Mulberry Street.
(© Tim Green)

Victorian half-crown, 1885.
(© Jerry Woody)

Victorian florin, 1875.
(© Jerry Woody)

William O'Brien MP
(unknown photographer).

at the ball was arrested, with the exception of a blind accordionist. Mass hearings followed at the Manchester Police Court, on Minshull Street, where many of the accused (who had initially been denied bail) had little option but to appear in their full Victorian female attire. Hundreds of ordinary Mancunians tried to view the proceedings from inside the court, and hundreds more blocked traffic in Minshull Street as they sought to view the accused entering and leaving the court building. The ball, and the subsequent police hearings, attracted national press attention, and the prejudicial, over-the-top news coverage was perhaps best summed up by the *Illustrated Police News* headline of 30 November 1880, which read 'Disgraceful Proceedings in Manchester – Men dressed as women'. The press, and indeed the magistrates in the court, had little idea of how to deal legitimately and compassionately with the largely taboo subject of homosexuality and (possible) male prostitution. Caminada gave evidence at the hearings, and was questioned at length by barristers representing many of the defendants. In the end, the arrested men were convicted of soliciting and/or incitement to commit improper actions, and they were released on the proviso that they paid two sureties of £25 each. The whole matter was forgotten about within a short period of time, and Caminada didn't make a single reference to the matter in his 1895 autobiographical book *25 Years of Detective Life*. It is only in comparatively recent times that the 1880 Temperance Hall Ball has been rescued from obscurity by writers celebrating the rich Lesbian, Gay, By-sexual and Transvestite (LGBT) history of Manchester.

Illustrated Police News, 1880.

Caminada could also handle the most discreet and sensitive of enquiries: for twenty-six years he was responsible for conducting delicate behind-the-scenes investigations into aspects of Irish nationalism, which entailed journeys to the USA, France, Germany and Ireland. When the Fenian dynamite conspiracies first became national news between 1881 and 1885, the detective was engaged in secret intelligence work which undoubtedly helped prevent a number of attacks and explosions in Manchester. In the modern era, police officers tend to be specialists, with detective squads focussing on murders, robberies, fraud and other matters. Caminada, however, was very much a generalist, a detective for all seasons and all cases, who was prepared to take on anything. Thus, when complaints reached Manchester police, in early 1888, about a man named Felix Rosenbaum maltreating a four-year-old boy in his custody, it was Chief Inspector Caminada who investigated the case. The story that Caminada uncovered was certainly a shocking one: Rosenbaum was a professional contortionist who lived in lodgings with the small boy. The boy's mother had given her child to Rosenbaum so that he could bring up the four-year-old as a 'bender' (a Victorian term for a professional contortionist). In order to 'train' the child, Rosenbaum beat his charge with considerable brutality, until the poor young boy could hardly walk. All this ended with Caminada's appearance on the scene. Rosenbaum was arrested for his cruelty, Caminada gave a detailed account of the case in court, and the adult bender received a well-deserved six months in prison, with hard labour. By the beginning of 1899, Jerome Caminada was a giant of both Manchester and British policing; a veteran policeman who'd seen and done it all. Yet, he certainly had his detractors, and he'd been openly criticised in an 1897 Home Office inquiry into Manchester policing, when it was revealed that Caminada had owned his own profitable public house (while being a serving officer) called the Shepherd's Bush Beerhouse. In addition, by the end of the 1890s, Manchester's leading detective was often at odds with the city's councillors, and with the Police Watch Committee – made up of magistrates and councillors – which oversaw the running of the local constabulary. It was probably a relief to both parties when Caminada's resignation letter was received and accepted by Manchester's Police Watch Committee in January 1899. However, if Watch Committee members thought that Caminada would disappear into a quiet retirement, they were in for a considerable surprise. The Manchester officer made the transition from being a policeman to a successful private detective with considerable ease. His work as a private detective continued to be reported upon, and he appeared in some highly publicised court cases. The ex-detective invested in properties in Rusholme and Moss Side, and became an Independent local councillor representing the Openshaw ward. His two autobiographical works – covering his police career and published in 1895 and 1910 – also sold well. By the time of his death in 1914, Jerome Caminada was a very wealthy man, and left an estate valued at over £16,000 (roughly equivalent to about £2,000,000 in 2022).

Victorian contortionist in action.
(© Wellcome Images)

Caminada family grave, Southern
Cemetery. (© Cnbrb)

MURDER, MADNESS AND CONFESSIONS

If murder was a comparatively rare occurrence in Manchester during the period 1850–1950, double murders were even more uncommon. When a man or woman committed two or more murders, national press attention was often intense and long-lasting. Charles Peace, born in Sheffield in 1832, was certainly one of the most written about, and notorious, of Victorian killers. His villainous life and escapades were the stuff of legend, and the subject of many penny dreadful novels, ballads and newspaper reports. Peace was certainly an enigma – a diminutive, maimed burglar who endured eighteen months in hospital as a fourteen year old, after suffering a horrific workplace injury when a white-hot steel rod penetrated his thigh and shattered his kneecap.

Charles Peace. (© Harvard School Library)

Despite his injuries as a youth, Peace proved to be an energetic, resourceful criminal, possessed of a charm and charisma which made him irresistible to many Victorian women. His connections with Manchester went back a long way, to at least the late 1850s, when he was sentenced to six years imprisonment for burgling a house in Rusholme. By the mid-1870s, Peace had spent over eighteen years in prison for burglaries and other serious offences committed in various locations around the country. By February 1876, however, he was free and back in Manchester, where he attempted yet another burglary. At around midnight on 11 February 1876, Peace attempted to burgle a mansion in Whalley Range, occupied by a Mr Gratrix. He was armed with a loaded revolver as he broke into the property. A young Manchester police constable named Nicholas Cock had spotted Peace as he went through Gratrix's entrance gate, and followed him in. Unfortunately for PC Cock, the ever-alert Charles Peace had realised he was being followed. The burglar fled from the Gratrix mansion, and shot the constable at close range before he escaped. Cock died shortly afterwards at a nearby doctor's house. The fatal shooting had taken place in complete darkness, and no one at all had been aware of Charles Peace's presence. Subsequently, three Irish brothers – John, William and Frank Habron – who lived near to the crime scene were questioned about the murder, and John and William Habron were put on trial for PC Cock's slaying. At the conclusion of the two-day Manchester Assizes trial, John was acquitted, but William was found guilty and sentenced to death. Charles Peace had managed to observe the whole trial from the anonymity of the public gallery, in order to check that no one at all linked him with the crime. He'd also taken time out from the trial in order to seduce the court secretary, Prudence Simpson, presumably in an effort to double check that the name of Charles Peace was in no way associated with the PC Cock murder. William Habron's youth (he was eighteen at the time of his conviction) ultimately led to his death sentence being commuted into one of life imprisonment. Habron might well have languished in gaol for decades had Peace not been arrested for other crimes committed in London and Sheffield. In October 1878, the Sheffield born killer was detained by police in London after wounding two officers during the attempted robbery of a house in Blackheath. Peace was sentenced to life imprisonment for these crimes, but was later taken north to stand trial for the murder of a man named Arthur Dyson, in Sheffield. Charles Peace had shot Dyson twice in the head, shortly after his return from witnessing Habron's trial in Manchester. The unfortunate Dyson had objected to Peace's attempts to seduce his wife, Martha, on many occasions, and he paid for these objections with his life. Charles Peace was convicted of Dyson's murder at Leeds Assizes in February 1879, and it was as he awaited execution in the condemned cell at Armley gaol that Peace confessed to the earlier murder of Nicholas Cock in Manchester. A much relieved William Habron was released from custody and given the enormous sum of £1000 in compensation for his wrongful arrest and conviction.

Right: Front cover of Charles
Peace penny dreadful novel.
(© Project Gutenberg eBook)

Below: Armley Gaol, Leeds. (© Rick Carn)

To an extent though, the Habrons were the authors of their own misfortunes: the brothers had clashed with, and threatened, PC Cock on previous occasions, and they had also concocted false alibies for themselves which were easily disproved. For instance, the brothers claimed they were all in bed by 9 p.m. on the night of Cock's murder. In reality, they were all drinking in an alehouse at 11 p.m., just a short distance away from where the policeman was murdered. These factors certainly helped reduce the credibility of the Habrons with members of the jury. Manchester police also placed far too much reliance on suspect boot print evidence, which allegedly placed William Habron at the scene of the crime. In the end, it was only Charles Peace's confession to the crime of killing PC Cock that allowed a terrible miscarriage of justice to finally be corrected. Just seven years after Charles Peace's confession ended the controversy surrounding PC Cock's killing, Manchester was convulsed by a very different but equally dramatic story of murder, love, money and family betrayal, which ended In Mary Ann Britland becoming the first woman to be hanged at Strangeways prison, on 9 August 1886. Mary Britland (née Hague) was an apparently hard-working woman who laboured as a factory operative during the day and a barmaid at night. She lived with her husband and youngest daughter, Elizabeth Hannah, at No. 133 Turner's Lane in Ashton-under-Lyne, which was some 6 miles to the east of central Manchester. In February 1886, Mrs Britland bought a quantity of mixed arsenic and strychnine labelled as 'Mr Harrison's Vermin Killer' from a chemist in Hulme, ostensibly to eradicate a mouse infestation at her Turner's Lane home. Even in the 1880s, these substances were recognised as being deadly in the wrong hands, and Mary was required to sign a poisons register. Mary Britland went on to buy quantities of strychnine 'mouse powder' on two further occasions in the coming months. In fact, at her subsequent trial for murder, an expert witness for the prosecution claimed that Mary had bought enough poison to kill all the mice in Ashton. On 9 March 1886, nineteen-year-old Elizabeth Britland died a sudden and terrible death, writhing in agony, and suffering from diarrhoea, vomiting and spasms. A complaisant doctor attributed the girl's death to natural causes, and her mother collected a £10 payment for a life insurance policy taken out in her daughter's name. On 3 May, Mary's husband, Thomas, died unexpectedly after a short illness, during which time he'd exhibited many of the same symptoms as his daughter. On this occasion, a doctor attributed his death to epilepsy. Shortly afterwards, his wife collected a combined £20 payment from Thomas's life insurance policy, and various other burial club subscriptions. The newly bereaved wife and mother was then invited to live with Thomas and Mary Dixon, who lived nearby at No. 128 Turner's Lane. Mary Britland and Thomas Dixon worked at the same factory during the day and were almost certainly engaged in a secret love affair. Very conveniently for Mary Britland, on 13 May, after eating a hearty supper, Mary Dixon became very ill, and died during the course of the following day. Mrs Dixon exhibited all the (by now) familiar symptoms of vomiting and spasms that had been observed just prior to

Victorian arsenic bottle. (© Wellcome Images)

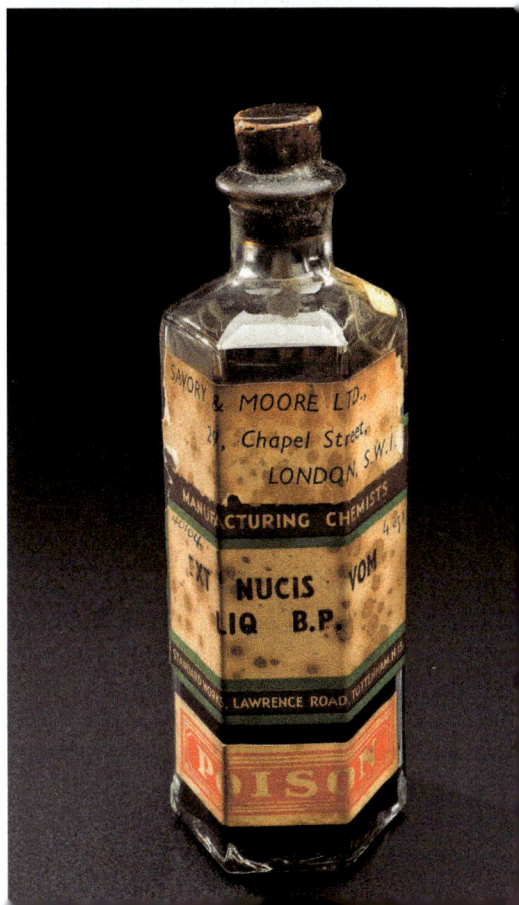

Victorian strychnine (nux vomica) bottle.
(© Wellcome Images)

the deaths of Elizabeth and Thomas Britland. Suspicious neighbours called in the police, and both Mary Britland and Thomas Dixon were arrested for murder. Mr Dixon was soon released, but Mary Ann Britland was charged with the murders of her daughter Elizabeth, her husband Thomas, and Mary Dixon.

Despite the fact that abnormally large amounts of arsenic and strychnine were found in the exhumed bodies of Thomas, Elizabeth and Mary Dixon, Mary Britland was indicted and tried at Manchester Assizes for the murder of just Mary Dixon. The eminent judge Edward Parry was an eyewitness to the whole trial, and observed that the deaths of Thomas and Elizabeth Britland were used by the prosecution in order to prove that Mary Britland had a definite method for murdering people via the administration of poison. This rather controversial tactic made it difficult for the defence to argue that the poison had been administered to Mary Dixon by accident. Even so, the prosecution tactic might well have backfired. At the end of the two-day trial, it took the jury over four hours to return a verdict of guilty against Mrs Britland. The jury also returned on two occasions to seek further directions from the trial judge, Mr Justice Cave. Nevertheless, after the verdict, Cave still donned the traditional black cap, and sentenced Mary Britland to death for the murder of Mrs Dixon. Her execution at Strangeways proved to be a rather horrific affair. Mary Britland was dragged to the gallows, screaming for mercy, by two female warders, and was then restrained by two burly male warders as she was positioned over the gallows trap door, and the rope was put over her neck. The executed woman was thirty-nine years old at the time of her death, and almost certainly, she had killed on multiple occasions for relatively modest financial gains, and in order to rid herself of a rival for Thomas Dixon's affections.

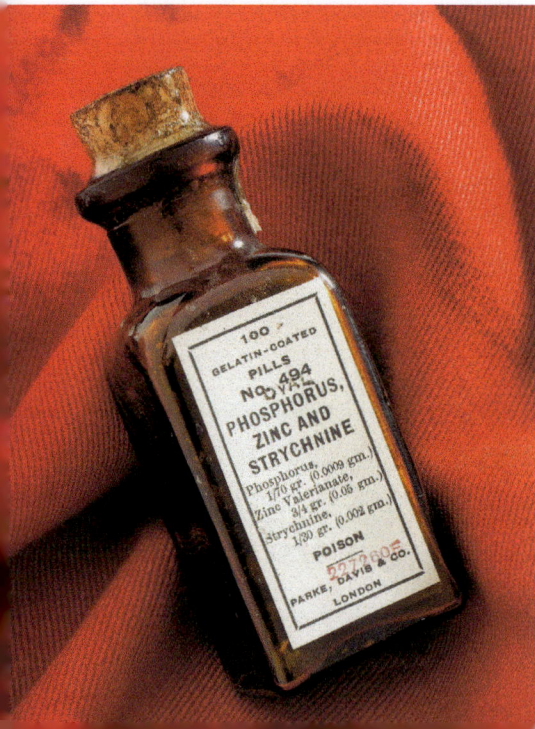

Phosphorus, zinc and strychnine poison pill bottle. (© Wellcome Images)

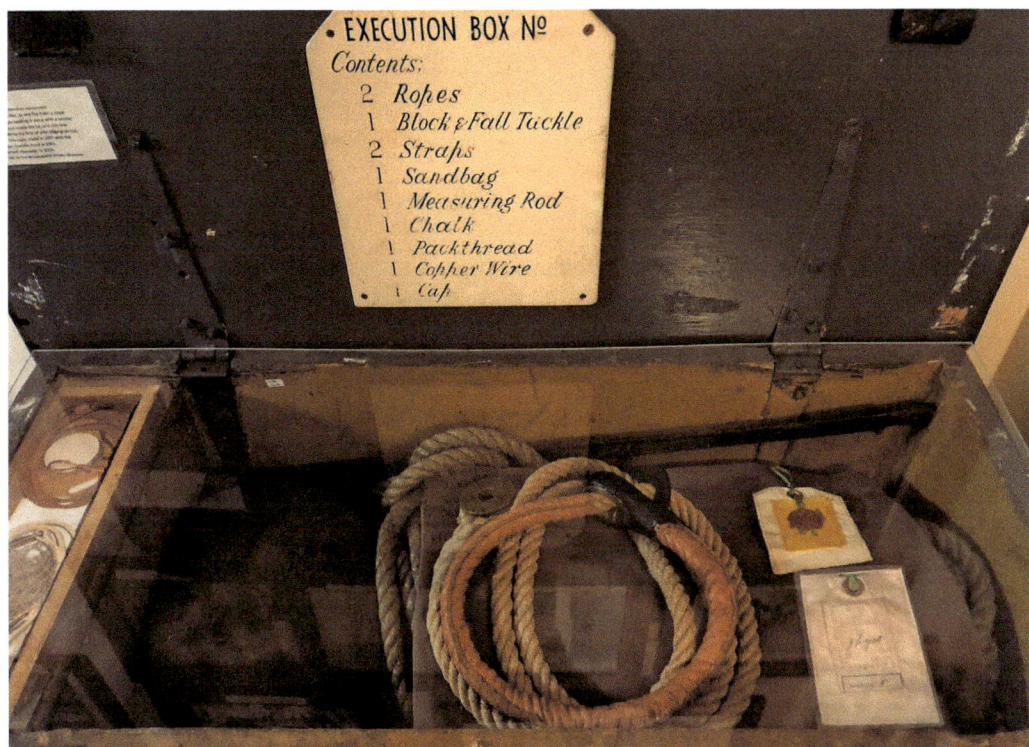

Hangman's execution box. (© SchroCat)

THE GEORGE FRATSON CASE

On 4 May 1929, a seventy-year-old hosier named George Armstrong was found dead in his shop at Grange Terrace, on Wilmslow Road in Rusholme. Armstrong had severe head injuries, blood covered the nearby walls, and the dead man's pockets had been searched and emptied. Theft and robbery had clearly been the motives for the crime, and Manchester police offered a £50 reward for information which led to the arrest and conviction of Armstrong's murderer. On 10 May 1929, George Fratson, a thirty-year-old cotton piecer of no fixed abode, was arrested on a minor charge in Preston. He was subsequently questioned by Manchester police about the Armstrong murder (for reasons which aren't entirely clear) and made fifteen statements to police about Armstrong's killing, which ended with him allegedly confessing to the crime. In July 1929, Fratson was tried for Armstrong's murder at Manchester Assizes, found guilty, and sentenced to death. After sentence was pronounced, George Fratson publicly proclaimed his innocence from the dock, just before he disappeared into the cells below the courtroom. In his statements to police, Fratson admitted visiting Armstrong's shop, but said that he never actually entered the premises. Fratson's defence team, led by the prominent Manchester barrister Harry Allan, launched an immediate appeal against the sentence. When the Court of Criminal Appeal met a few weeks after Fratson's conviction, Allan produced a new piece of evidence – a battered cardboard collar box from Armstrong's shop containing a bloodstained fingerprint which didn't belong to either Armstrong or George Fratson. Despite this new evidence, the Court of Appeal still dismissed Fratson's case. However, the head of Scotland Yard's fingerprint bureau was called in to look at the new evidence, and George Fratson's sentence was commuted into one of life imprisonment. The belief in some quarters that Fratson might well be innocent of the crime seemed to be gaining some momentum, and the Home Secretary, John Clynes, became involved when he asked the Court of Criminal Appeal to again review the Fratson case. Clynes's decision meant that for the first time in British legal history there was to be a rehearing of an appeal against a murder conviction. George Fratson's hopes of a pardon were dashed, however, when the Court of Criminal Appeal dismissed his second appeal, on 25 March 1930. Fratson remained in prison, and he stayed either behind bars or in a secure hospital for the next thirty-two years. From the moment that his death sentence was commuted, there seemed at least some prospect of the ex-cotton worker being pardoned, or at least released on parole. The fact that this hope was never realised almost certainly preyed on Fratson's mind, and he became mentally ill. As a result, he was transferred to Broadmoor Hospital in Berkshire (referred to at the time as the Broadmoor Criminal Lunatic Asylum) in the early 1930s. Fratson's very last hope of freedom came in 1934, when a man named Walter Prince claimed that he had killed George Armstrong. Prince made this confession while standing trial for murder at Nottingham Assizes, and these startling revelations made newspaper headlines across the UK. Unfortunately for Fratson, no firm evidence could be found which tied Prince to the Armstrong

John Clynes, Home Secretary 1929–31. (© Bain News Service)

Above: *Illustrated London News'* depiction of Broadmoor. (© Wellcome Images)

Below: Plan of men's block at Broadmoor, *c.* 1885. (© Wellcome Images)

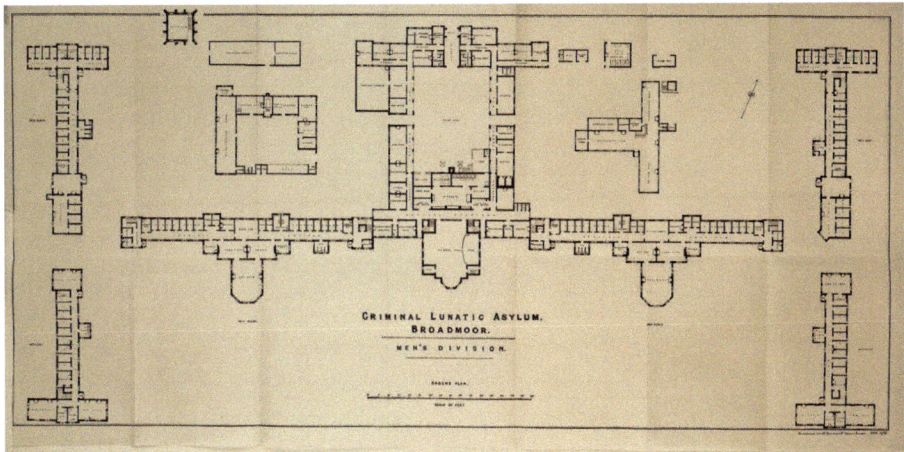

murder. In any event, Prince was found guilty of murder at his trial, and then promptly declared insane. He retracted his confession to the Armstrong murder, and joined Fratson as a patient at Broadmoor Hospital. George Fratson made an abortive attempt to escape from Broadmoor in 1948, and was eventually released on parole in 1962. By this stage, however, he was struggling with severe mental illness and probably incapable of coping with the outside world. He was soon back inside Broadmoor, though he was later transferred to a psychiatric hospital in Colchester, where he stayed until his death in 1981. In early August 1967, in an action touched with considerable pathos, Fratson absconded temporarily from his Colchester hospital and travelled to Manchester. He told hospital and police authorities that he was launching one last effort to track down the real killer of George Armstrong. Police officers found 'old George', as Fratson was then known, in an unnamed Manchester hostel, and with considerable courtesy, they then took him back to Colchester.

POLITICAL CRIMES

For the Victorian period at least, the city of Manchester was viewed by many as being the crime capital of Great Britain. Laws were transgressed for a whole host of different reasons from lust and avarice to dire financial necessity and hunger. Alcoholic intoxication fuelled many crimes, and for many violent youth scuttler gang crimes, there was often no real cause other than a basic tribal loyalty to particular streets and a need to be seen as being tough and hard in front of friends and fellow gang members. Politically motivated crimes were, however, in a category of their own: those who broke the law because of their belief in a political cause weren't motivated by thoughts of personal gain or advantage, and for roughly seventy years between the 1860s and the 1930s, Manchester had a particularly wide variety of politically motivated law breakers.

THE FENIANS

The 1851 census calculated that the population of Manchester stood at 400,000. Of this number, 52,500 were Irish born. The new Irish arrivals in Manchester tended to congregate in particular areas, so that by 1861, for example, 50 per cent of all those that lived in the slum district of Angel Meadow (when children are included) had been born in Ireland. New Irish arrivals lived in the worst accommodation and took on the poorest paid jobs. Even so, relations with English born Mancunians tended to be rather fractious. The uneasy relationship between some members of the Irish community, and other Mancunians, was made worse in the 1860s by the increasing popularity of the Irish Republican Brotherhood (IRB), otherwise known as the Fenians. The IRB had been founded in 1858, as a revolutionary organisation dedicated to the creation of an independent Irish republic, by force of arms, and many of the new Irish immigrants to Manchester were adherents to its cause. IRB sinews had been stiffened by an influx of Irish American officers with military experience gained in the American Civil War. These militarily experienced soldiers became leaders in the IRB, and were instrumental in organising a Fenian uprising in Ireland during 1867. The rising itself proved to be something of a damp squib, quickly ignited and quickly suppressed, and the Irish American Fenian leader, Colonel Thomas Kelly, accompanied by Captain Timothy Deasy (one of his principal lieutenants) had little option but to flee to England. It was entirely logical and predictable that Kelly and Deasy's first action would be to visit Manchester, with its huge Irish born population, in order to drum up further support for the Fenian cause. The two men were, however, captured by Manchester police after a Fenian meeting in Shudehill, and remanded in custody to Belle Vue prison. News of Kelly and

Colonel Thomas Joseph Kelly
(unknown photographer).

Deasy's capture in Manchester soon reached America, and one of the men's ex-Civil War comrades, Thomas O'Meagher Condon, raced to Britain to try and secure their freedom. Condon recruited an armed gang of Fenian supporters to try and rescue Kelly and Deasy, and on 17 September 1867, this group ambushed a horse-drawn Black Maria police van carrying Kelly, Deasy and other prisoners from a remand hearing back to Belle Vue prison. The Fenian gang opened fire on the police van just as it was passing under a railway bridge on Hyde Road, and Police Sergeant Charles Brett was shot dead in the ensuing struggle to free Kelly and Deasy. Brett was inside the van, with the prisoners, when he received a fatal bullet wound to the head, fired from outside by an unknown Fenian assailant. As a result, Sergeant Brett became the very first in a long line of Manchester police officers to be killed on duty. Both Kelly and Deasy were freed successfully by the Fenian raiders, and managed to escape from Britain. Members of the gang that freed them were, however, not quite so lucky. The rumpus at the police van attracted quite a large crowd of ordinary Mancunians, who pursued and captured a number of the Fenian gang responsible for freeing Kelly and Deasy. Among those seized by the Manchester mob were five men who were later to stand trial for the murder of Sergeant Charles Brett. The five men were Thomas Condon, the instigator of the rescue, a nineteen-year-old carpenter named William Allen, Michael Larkin, who was a married tailor with five children, Michael O'Brien, and Michael Maguire. All five men were found guilty of Brett's murder, despite the fact that no one knew who had fired the fatal shot, and

Above: Victorian horse-drawn black maria police van. (© George Grantham Bain Collection)

Left: Charles Brett. (© GMP Museum)

all five were sentenced to death. Subsequently, Condon's American citizenship helped save him from the gallows, and Maguire was given a pardon when it became clear (despite the court's guilty verdict) that he'd had nothing to do with the actual killing of Brett. There was to be no last-minute reprieve, though, for Allen, Larkin and O'Brien. All three men were hanged, publicly, outside Salford's New Bailey prison, in a multiple execution witnessed by between 8,000 and 10,000 people. Allen, Larkin and O'Brien went to their deaths with considerable stoicism and fortitude. They refused to say who had actually fired the shot that killed Brett, but were still convicted of murder as a 'joint enterprise' by a special commission presided over by the Lord Chancellor of Ireland, Justice Blackthorne, along with Mr Justice Mellor. Allen, Larkin and O'Brien's undoubted courage at both their trial and execution, and their unwavering loyalty to the political cause they served, excited much admiration and sympathy across the world (and not just in Irish nationalist circles). They became known as the Manchester Martyrs, and their activities have been the focus of much historical attention ever since. This focus has, however, served to obscure the equally sad story of Police Sergeant Charles Brett. The 1860s were a time of considerable anti-Irish

The Manchester Martyrs, *c.* 1893. (© Popular Grafic Arts)

prejudice in Manchester, and elsewhere. Irish immigrants were often believed to be fuelling crime waves, and to be undercutting the wages of English workers. It is sadly ironic, but these prejudicial viewpoints were almost certainly not shared by Charles Brett. At the time of his violent death in 1867, Brett was in his early fifties, a father of four, and a policeman who'd worked for over sixteen years in the constabularies of Macclesfield and Manchester. More pertinently, in the aftermath of the Irish potato famine, when millions of Irish economic migrants flocked to England, Charles Brett and his family had taken in Irish lodgers. The 1851 census, for example, records that Charles and his wife Mary gave a home in Macclesfield to three Irish female boot binders. The presence of these three women, probably taken under the wing of Mary Brett, may well indicate that Charles Brett and his family had a reasonably tolerant attitude to the whole question of Irish immigration. Unfortunately, Charles Brett's opinions about the Irish were of no real interest to the Fenians, who shot him dead during their successful rescue of Thomas Kelly and Captain Deasy.

THE SUFFRAGETTES

The term 'suffragette' was originally coined by the *Daily Mail* newspaper during 1906, and was intended as a derogatory reference to those women who campaigned for the right to vote, with increasing militancy, during the first years of the twentieth century. The label of being a 'suffragette' was adopted by women who campaigned for the suffrage to be extended to women as well as men, and to a very great extent, Manchester became the spiritual home of this campaign to extend voting rights to females. It became the spiritual home of the suffragette movement because of the activities of the Pankhurst family, who resided at No. 21 Nelson Street, Rusholme, in Manchester. The matriarch of the family was Emmeline, who had three daughters – Christobel, Sylvia and Adela – who all, in their different ways, promoted the cause of women's suffrage. Traditionally, the Manchester Pankhursts have been seen as being right at the core of the nationwide women's suffrage movement. In recent decades, however, the historiography of the voting rights for women campaign has shed light on the importance of other groups such as the National Union of Women's Suffrage Societies and the Women's Freedom League, which weren't dominated by the Pankhurst women. Even so, the Pankhurst women, particularly Emmeline and her eldest daughter Christobel, were of crucial importance to the overall voting rights campaign. In 1903, Emmeline founded the Women's Social and Political Union (WSPU) in Manchester, which rapidly became the most militant of all the various women's suffrage groups. The question of when the British suffragette movement really became militant in its quest for female voting rights has always aroused some uncertainty. Emmeline believed militancy began in May 1905, when she launched a WSPU protest outside Westminster Abbey, when parliament failed to allocate time for discussion and passage of a Women's Enfranchisement Bill. In reality though, women's suffrage militancy really began in Manchester, in October 1905,

Above: Pankhurst family home in Nelson Street, Manchester. © Kurt Adkins)

Right: Emmeline Pankhurst, *c*. 1913. (© Library of Congress)

Sylvia Pankhurst. (© Bain News)

when Christobel Pankhurst, along with her friend and colleague Annie Kenney, caused a disturbance at a Liberal Party rally at the Manchester Free Trade Hall. There were distinguished speakers at the event, including Sir Edward Grey and Winston Churchill, and the smooth flow of sonorous speeches and enthusiastic applause was brought to a shuddering halt when a gutsy Christobel and Annie Kenney leapt up and began questioning speakers about whether or not they supported votes for women. The two women were ejected rapidly from the main meeting hall and detained in an adjoining room until the police arrived. During the period of her detention, Christobel managed to either slap or hit a witness to the events in the main hall, and when her arms were pinned behind her by a member of the constabulary, she spat at a policeman (an act which constituted a technical assault). When she appeared before magistrates, accused of assault and causing a disturbance, Christobel claimed she thought the policemen were members of the Liberal Party, and not members of the constabulary (which caused considerable laughter in the court). She was found guilty by the presiding magistrates and fined. Christobel refused to pay the fine and was subsequently sentenced to seven days imprisonment. The whole event was a publicity godsend for Christobel and the WSPU. Membership numbers shot up, and by February 1907 the WSPU had forty-seven branches and nine paid organisers. Christobel and Annie Kenney's motivation for committing their various misdemeanours at the Manchester Free Trade Hall was entirely political, and the results (at least for the WSPU) were very positive indeed.

Above: Manchester's Free Trade Hall.
(© Bernt Rostad)

Right: Edward Grey, by Bassano.

Winston Churchill in 1906
(unknown photographer).

Christobel Pankhurst in 1910.
(© LSE Library)

Annie Kenney in 1909.
(© Bain News Service)

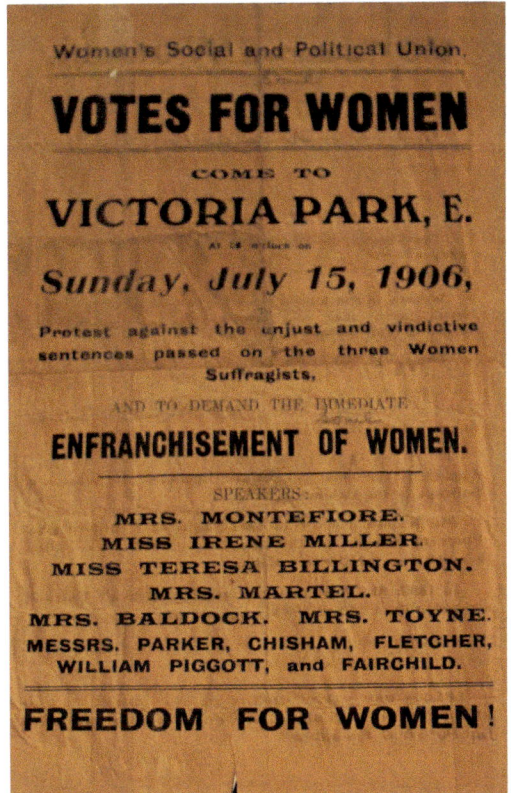

Victoria Park WSPU meeting, 1906.
(© People's History Museum)

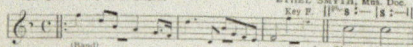
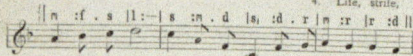
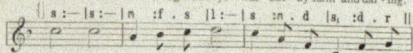
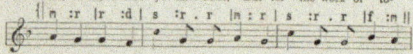
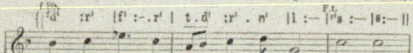
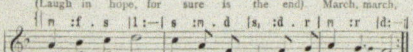

March of the Women, sung at WSPU rallies, *c.* 1911. (© www.bl.ukcollection)

Suffragettes boycotting 1911 census in Manchester. (© Johnny Cyprus)

By 1908, suffragette militancy had escalated to encompass attacks on private property, and by 1912 arson attacks and bombing of private properties were being undertaken by committed suffragettes. Manchester suffragettes played a significant part in these increasingly militant activities. In April 1913, three suffragettes from the Manchester area were charged with maliciously damaging thirteen paintings at the Manchester Art Gallery, on Mosley Street. Lillian Forrester lived on Grosvenor Road in Whalley Range, and was the thirty-four-year-old wife of a successful local chemical analyst, Evelyn Manestra was a governess, and also lived on Grosvenor Road, while Anne Briggs came from the Rochdale area. All three women were detained by attendants after they'd tried to smash some of the gallery's most valuable paintings, which were all located in the Central Room – sometimes called Room No. 4 – of the institution. Pre-Raphaelite paintings fared particularly badly at the hands of the suffragettes, with roughly £200 worth of damage being done to G. F. Watts' *The Servant*. The glass frames were smashed in a selection of other paintings, and a 2-inch hole was made in the glass panelling encasing Rossetti's *Astarte and Syriaca*, though the canvas itself remained undamaged. Gallery officials calculated that replacing the smashed glass alone (in all the targetted paintings) would cost about £170. The motivation for the

Manchester Art Gallery. (© Pemolo)

Left: *Astarte Syriaca*, 1877, by Dante Gabriel Rossetti (1828–82).

Right: Lillian Forrester in prison. (© National Archives)

Manchester Art Gallery attacks was entirely political. When questioned, Evelyn Manestra objected to being charged with causing 'malicious' damage, because her actions were done for political reasons, rather than for reasons of malice. Lillian Forrester's stated reasons for destroying paintings were different, but also political. She sought to publicise what she saw as the state's unfair and brutal treatment of Emmeline Pankhurst, who had recently been imprisoned for being involved in a bomb attack on a Surrey property belonging to Lloyd George. The political character of the Manchester Art Gallery attacks was also summed up by the small cards that Forrester and Manestra left behind, attached to a hammer, amid the glass shards and other wreckage in the Central Room. On one side was written the comment 'Dishonourable men in parliament, honourable women in prison'. On the other side was written the comment 'end forced feeding now,' which was an obvious reference to the prison practice of forcibly feeding jailed suffragettes who were on hunger strike. Both Lillian Forrester and Evelyn Manestra were jailed for the damage they caused at the Manchester Art Gallery. Annie Briggs, who said nothing at all when questioned by police, was eventually acquitted. Lillian Forrester died three years later, in 1916. Whether or not the militancy she exhibited amongst the Pre-Raphaelite masterpieces at the Manchester Art Gallery actually helped advance the cause of women's suffrage is perhaps open to question. At least some historians of the women's suffrage movement feel that suffragette militancy, after 1912, hindered rather than helped the passage of equal voting rights legislation. In the end, these revisionist historians believe that it was the formation of alliances between women's suffrage bodies and elements in the Liberal, Conservative and fast-emerging Labour Party that did most to smooth the way towards equal voting rights for women between 1918 and 1928.

DON'T SHOOT!

The few years immediately prior to the outbreak of the First World War were ones of increasing political and industrial unrest in Britain. At the same time as the suffragettes were launching arson and bomb attacks across Britain, opposition to Home Rule for Ireland was becoming increasingly vociferous, Liverpool dockers were embroiled in a bitter trade dispute, and miners had downed tools across the country in 1912. The uneasy political and industrial situation led a number of pioneering trade unionist and Independent Labour Party radicals to believe that the Liberal government of the time might use the military to crack down on industrial militancy. Tom Mann was a towering figure in the development of British trade unionism, and of the Labour Party. By 1912, he was president of a body called the Industrial Syndicalised Education League, which produced one issue of *The Syndicalist* newspaper every month. In early January 1912, *The Syndicalist* produced an article (without comment) entitled an 'Open Letter to British Soldiers', written by an anonymous member of the Liverpool construction trades. In this letter, the writer urged British soldiers not to obey the orders of their superior officers, if they were ordered to intervene in any way against workers during an industrial dispute. The letter was often summed up as being the 'Don't Shoot' article, and Mann made speeches at Salford and Pendleton Town Halls, during March 1912, in which he passionately supported the sentiments expressed in the Open Letter. After making these speeches, Mann returned to his

Tom Mann (1856–1941).

home in Wimbledon, where he was soon arrested by Scotland Yard detectives, under a warrant issued by Salford police. Tom Mann was actually arrested for contravening the terms of the 1797 Incitement to Mutiny Act, which had originally been passed in the aftermath of the Nore and Spithead naval mutinies, when large parts of the Royal Navy had refused to obey the commands of their superior officers. Although by 1912 the original Act was 115 years old, and might be considered to be rather archaic, it could still be used to prosecute anyone considered guilty of encouraging members of the British armed forces to disobey the orders of their superior officers. After being arrested, Mann was taken to Cannon Row police station in London, and spent the night in police cells, where he had a long visit from Keir Hardie, the prominent Labour leader. On the following morning, he was taken north to Manchester, via train, accompanied by police officers. Much later in the day, he appeared in front of stipendiary magistrate Spencer Hogg, at Salford Police Court (situated in the Town Hall), having been formally charged with three offences – one misdemeanour and two more serious felonies – under the terms of the Incitement to Mutiny Act. At this first hearing, bail was refused, and Mann was remanded in custody. Only at a second hearing,

Open letter
to British
soldiers, 1912.

a week later, was the socialist firebrand finally given bail, and he eventually stood trial at Manchester Assizes, on the charges of Incitement to Mutiny, in May 1912. Tom Mann conducted his own defence at his highly publicised trial. The presiding judge, Justice Bankes, certainly seems to have given Mann a fair hearing, and even provided the defendant with a small table in the dock so that the radical activist could make his own notes as the trial progressed. Even so, the jury seems to have had no real difficulties in finding Mann guilty of incitement, and Justice Bankes sentenced Tom Mann to six months' imprisonment, in the 'second division' at Strangeways prison. Incarceration in the second division meant that Mann escaped the necessity of undergoing hard labour whilst in prison. Suffragette literature of the time constantly complained about suffrage activists being imprisoned in the 'third division', which meant that they were subject to hard labour and were treated like ordinary female felons. Mann escaped all this controversy in the second division, and was released from custody after serving just seven weeks of his sentence. This difference in sentencing policy, between Mann and many of the imprisoned suffragettes, certainly casts an interesting light on judicial attitudes of the time.

FASCISTS

Manchester was again the scene of much politically motivated law breaking during the 1930s, this time precipitated by the actions of Sir Oswald Mosley's far right British Union of Fascists, who marched through the streets of the city, and held rallies, with some regularity, between 1933 and 1939. The highly controversial Mosley, born in 1896, and the son of a baronet, began his political life as a Conservative MP, at the young age of twenty-one. He then transferred his allegiance to the Labour Party, and became Chancellor of the Duchy of Lancaster during Ramsay Macdonald's administration. Mosley then quit the Labour Party when his proposals for tackling Britain's economic problems during the Great Depression were rejected. A highly frustrated Mosley subsequently formed his own political party, rather unimaginatively called the New Party, which wasn't a great success. After visiting Mussolini's fascist Italy in 1932, Mosley returned to Britain, where he set up the British Union of Fascists (BUF). The BUF incorporated the authoritarian and totalitarian characteristics of Mussolini's fascists and Hitler's Nazi Party, with no internal party democracy, and a Blackshirt defence force who were free with their fists and always keen and willing to pitch into fights with political opponents. As the 1930s progressed, the BUF also developed a particularly virulent antisemitism. In general, the BUF's activities in London are well known. Its brutal treatment of any opposition at the party's 1934 Olympia rally received considerable press attention at the time, as did the BUF Blackshirts' struggles with anti-fascist opponents during the Battle of Cable Street in 1936. Less has been written about the BUF's attempts to promote itself in Manchester and the north-west, which to some extent mirrored events in London, and also led to street battles and fascist and anti-fascist protestors appearing in court for

Left: Oswald Mosley and bride, 1920.
(© Bain Collection)

Below: Mosley and family on holiday in
1929. (© Rudyard Kipling123)

a variety of mostly low-level public order offences. The BUF certainly had its supporters in Manchester and the north-west, and was therefore able to host a number of well attended rallies, and other events, in the area during the 1930s. Mosley, for example, spoke at a packed BUF rally at the Manchester Free Trade Hall during March 1933 – an event marshalled by aggressive truncheon-wielding fascist Blackshirt stewards. There was an equally well attended and violent BUF rally at the same venue in November 1934. Large numbers of fascist supporters also attended a BUF rally at Belle Vue in October 1933, and over 5,000 people gathered to hear Mosley speak at Albert Croft in Collyhurst on 19 July 1936. Nevertheless, BUF support can certainly be exaggerated. Nationally, perhaps 100,000 people passed through its ranks during the whole period of its existence (the organisation was banned in 1940) and most recruits only stayed as members for short periods. In 1938, an internal BUF estimate suggested that there were only 3,500 active party members throughout the entire UK, and fascist support was always much greater in London than elsewhere. Many of those that attended BUF meetings and rallies in Manchester did so in order to protest against them, and consequently found themselves appearing in front of Manchester Police Court, charged with misdemeanours such as disorderly behaviour and obstructing and assaulting police officers. Lilly Clyne, for example, was a seventeen-year-old girl from Waterloo Road in Cheetham, who was arrested for disorderly behaviour and obstructing police during skirmishes with Blackshirts at the BUF Manchester Free Trade Hall meeting of 25 November 1934. She was almost certainly at the event with her father, protesting against Mosley's meeting, and was arrested as she tried to prevent police from arresting and detaining her father. Both father and daughter were later found guilty by magistrates, and fined £1 and five shillings respectively. At the same sitting, magistrates also fined two men for behaving in a disorderly manner 'by shouting'. These men were almost certainly part of a group of several hundred Jewish residents who, according to a policeman at the scene, shouted 'down with the Blackshirts!' as fascist supporters left the Free Trade Hall meeting. These verbal insults then developed into a fight which police officers had to bring to an end. Rather incongruously, four protestors detained by fascist stewards inside the Free Trade Hall venue were later handed over to police and then charged with various offences on the basis of information and summonses supplied by the fascists themselves.

Some anti-fascist protestors were also charged with far more serious crimes than being merely disorderly, or obstructing the police: George Olsen Melander was a nineteen-year-old labourer from Walton, who attended Mosley's 10,000 strong fascist rally in Liverpool on 10 October 1937. Melander attended in order to protest against fascism, and threw a large stone in Mosley's direction as the BUF leader climbed a ladder in order to speak from the top of a van. The stone hit Mosley on the head, and he collapsed, unconscious, to the ground. Melander was subsequently arrested by police and charged with two counts of causing grievous bodily harm (GBH) to the leader of the BUF. The young labourer endured a much publicised trial at Manchester Assizes for these offences, in December 1937. Mosley gave evidence at the trial about his injuries, but after due deliberation the jury found Melander not guilty of intending to cause GBH, and they failed to agree a verdict on the question of whether Melander had caused actual GBH to the fascist leader (these charges were finally dropped in January 1938).

Left: BUF child's uniform jacket. (© Lee Wright)

Below: Fascist *Blackshirt* newspaper, October 1936. (© Zezen)

JEWEL THIEVES

Jewel thieves and jewel robberies have always had a particular hold on the imagination of many members of the British public. This was certainly the case during the century between 1850 and 1950, when Manchester's many jewel thefts were written about in considerable detail by newspapers across the length and breadth of the British Isles. Of course, jewels could be (and were) stolen from private houses, hotels, warehouses and railway stations. Predictably, however, it was from Manchester's many wholesale and retail jewellery businesses that the vast bulk of the city's valuable jewels were stolen. Many of the larger Manchester jewel robberies were referred to in the most dramatic and sensational terms by British newspapers. On 7 March 1853, for example, Howard's jewellers on Victoria Street was targetted by thieves in what the *Carlisle Patriot* newspaper described as being 'the cleverest and best executed robbery we have ever heard of in Manchester'. Later in the century, on 7 October 1898, *The Manchester Times* also referred to the 'daring jewel robbery of a most audacious character' which had just been carried out at the jewellery premises of Mr P. G. Powell in Market Street. The press in Manchester, and elsewhere, liked jewel robbery stories, and jewel thieves, because news about such things sold newspapers. The legendary status of the jewel thief in British national consciousness really reached its zenith at the end of the nineteenth century, and during Edwardian times, with the publication of E. W. Hornung's popular tales about the exploits of the clever, immaculately dressed jewel thief Raffles. This image of the appealing, dapper jewel thief was pursued even into the 1950s with Cary Grant's portrayal of the retired miscreant John Robie, in Hitchcock's film *To Catch a Thief*.

Victoria Street in 1860, from *Reminiscences of Manchester* by L. Hayes, 1905.

Above: Victoria Street, *c.* 1868–78. (© Rijksmuseum)

Below: Market Street in 1889. (© Ardfern)

Above: Raffles, played by Kyrle Bellew in 1904.
(© Sayre Collection of Theatrical Photographs)

Right: *To Catch a Thief* poster, 1955.
(© Paramount Pictures)

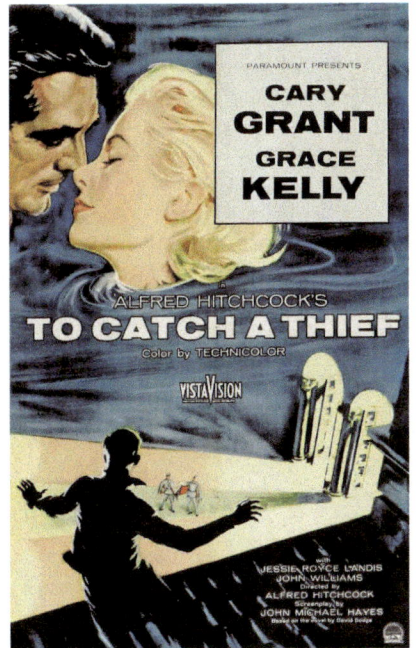

To an extent, some of Manchester's jewel thieves did fit in with these widely held popular conceptions, and were possessed of engaging personalities which appealed to both press and public alike. Edgar Payne (alias Lucky Edgar) was, for example, a roguish jewel thief, born in Ormskirk, who hit the national headlines in 1947 when he snatched over £10,000 of assorted jewellery from Margaret Foggarty, an assistant at Finnigan's jewellers of Deansgate, Manchester, as she was trying to close the store for the day. Lucky Edgar's haul was worth well over £400,000 in today's money. After grabbing the jewels, Edgar ran at top speed through the streets of Manchester, colliding with a handcart in the process and injuring his throat. Lucky was subsequently captured by a civilian, and not the police, and because of his throat injury, he was unable to speak at all during his first remand hearing. Not-so-lucky Edgar was remanded in custody to Strangeways gaol, and at a subsequent remand hearing he was the only prisoner in a police van that took him from Strangeways to Newton Street police station, prior to an appearance at the Manchester Police Court. Once the police van doors were opened, Edgar immediately shot out and sprinted down the nearest street. Two policemen chased after Edgar for over 400 yards, but the jewel thief outran them both. Manchester police then used their car radio systems to seal off all road exits from the city. Despite the best efforts of the Manchester constabulary, Edgar Payne made good his escape, and nothing was heard from him for the next two and a half years. In July 1950, the on-the-run jewel thief was arrested in Glasgow for possessing a forged identity card. Glasgow police were soon able to discover Payne's true identity, and he was taken back to Manchester to stand trial for the original 1947 Finnigan's jewel robbery. Lucky Edgar seemed quite philosophical on his return to Manchester's Victoria station, in handcuffs. He aimed a well-placed kick at a photographer trying to take his picture, but also had time to comment that his predicament was all the result (in his opinion) of having too many girlfriends. The Ormskirk jewel thief was later sentenced to nine months' imprisonment for his various wrong doings, which (all things considered) was undoubtedly quite a lenient punishment.

A number of the jewel robberies that took place in Manchester during the period 1850–1950 also stand out for their meticulous planning and careful attention to detail. In July 1865, for example, over £13,000 of gold and silver watches, rings, pins, bracelets, chains, lockets and other expensive items were stolen from W. M. Ferran's jewellery premises on Victoria Street, in central Manchester. *The Morning Post* of 20 July described the event as 'the greatest robbery ever known to have occurred in Manchester'. The robbers certainly took great pains to gain access to the ground floor of Ferran's shop, cutting their way through two 9-inch-thick walls in adjacent business premises, and then pushing their way through a third wall on the top floor of the Ferran's property. After the loot had been safely bagged, the thieves spent the night hiding in nearby offices, before disappearing onto Victoria Street early on the following morning. No one was arrested for the robbery, and none of the stolen items were ever

Right: Modern Deansgate. (© Steve Daniels)

Below: Former police station on Newton Street. (© Repton1x)

Above: Victoria Station. (© Paul Hermans)

Left: Tiled former entry for Victoria Station's first-class passengers. (© acediscovery)

recovered. Thirty-three years later, in 1898, *The Manchester Times* were probably quite justified in highlighting the 'audacious' nature of the already mentioned Powell's jewellery robbery on Market Street, in which thieves stole over £1,000 in assorted diamonds and expensive watches. Robbers gained access to Liston's bar and billiard room, which was situated above the Powell premises. Overnight, the thieves cut a small hole, measuring only 14 inches by 11 inches, through the billiard room floor into the jeweller's below. An umbrella was inserted through the small hole as it was being widened, and then opened so that plaster dropping from the ceiling could be caught silently within its folds, rather than clattering noisily to the floor. Possibly a small boy or girl then descended through the tiny gap, using a rope, in order to steal the rings and watches. The gang subsequently escaped through a rear window of the billiard room, and nothing was ever heard of them again.

Neither the Powell jewellery shop robbers, nor the Ferran's thieves, committed any acts of physical violence during the course of their crimes. Numerous other Manchester jewel robberies of the period, however, turned out to be quite brutish and violent. The 1853 robbery of Howard's, on Market Street, so lauded by the *Carlisle Patriot,* was certainly well planned, and roughly £13,000 of jewellery was stolen – equivalent to about £1,730,000 in 2022. The gang of (probably) four thieves certainly knew when to strike: they timed the robbery to take place between 1–2 p.m., when the shop owner and his chief assistant had both left the premises for lunch, leaving only eighteen-year-old Fanny Howard (the owner's daughter) to run the shop, while an errand boy toiled away in the cellar. The robbers, aided by a lookout described by the newspapers as being 'a flash dresser in the sporting style', then burst in, and poor Fanny was semi-garrotted into unconsciousness. Huge quantities of rings, watches and other items were stolen, and only two of the thieves were later caught. The 1874 robbery of L. S. Knight's, a jewellery wholesaler's in Shudehill, was another rather unsavoury, brutal affair. On this occasion, a three-man gang stole between £3,000 and £4,000 of assorted jewellery. The robbers, named Arthur Gaylor, Alfred Coyne and George Montague, were experienced thieves, wanted for a series of jewellery related crimes in Birmingham and elsewhere. The gang were aided by two women, Ann Henry and Jane Gray, who acted as lookouts, and were also responsible for storing and transporting the equipment needed for house-breaking and cracking open safes. Ann Henry was Coyne's common-law wife, and Jane Gray was the wife of Gaylor. Like a number of other Manchester jewel thieves, George Montague was also armed, on this occasion with a revolver, which he was clearly prepared to use. The Knight's Shudehill robbery proved to be the last one committed by Gaylor, Coyne and Montague for a very long time. The gang's presence in Manchester had been betrayed to police by an unknown informer. All public places and railway stations had been put under police surveillance, and the gang's presence in Shudehill was soon spotted. Ann Henry and Jane Gray were arrested, and police surrounded the premises of L. S. Knight's, where the gang were caught red-handed as they emerged with their stolen jewels and watches. Gaylor, Coyne and Montague didn't give up without a fight, however. All three men were injured, along with a number of policemen, in a brutal skirmish outside Knight's. During the kerfuffle, Montague was smashed to the ground as he pointed his revolver at one of the detectives trying to arrest him. All three criminals later received heavy sentences at the Manchester Assizes, with Montague receiving the heaviest term of fourteen years' imprisonment, principally because of his attempted use of a firearm. Arthur Gaylor went to prison for twelve years, Coyne for ten, and Gaylor's wife received a fifteen-month gaol term. Only Ann Henry got off relatively lightly, receiving a nine-month prison sentence.

The actions of some jewel thieves could also have unforeseen but tragic consequences. In May 1892, a wholesale jeweller from Birmingham called Michael Goldschmidt was selling his wares to fellow jewellers in Deansgate, when a gang of thieves snatched over £4,000 worth of his stock. Goldschmidt was so distraught at the loss of his various jewels that he returned to his hotel that evening and took his own life. The legendary Manchester detective Jerome Caminada was given the job of tracking down the culprits, and it took him nearly two years to identify two of the main thieves involved. One of the villains had escaped to America after the Deansgate theft, but later returned to Liverpool, where he'd been involved in a failed bank robbery. The man had been captured and sentenced to ten years in prison for the offence. George Jones was another of the Deansgate robbers. He'd fled to Ireland after the Deansgate snatch, and had served a one year sentence in Limerick gaol for an unnamed offence. After his release, Caminada brought Jones back to Manchester, where an eyewitness positively identified him as one of the men involved in stealing Michael Goldschmidt's precious jewellery items. Jones was later found guilty of the robbery, at Manchester Assizes, and sentenced to eighteen months in prison for the crime which led to Goldschmidt's untimely demise.

Although the archetypal jewel thief was undoubtedly a male in the public imagination, not all Manchester jewel thieves were men. Ann Henry and Jane Gray acted in the subservient capacity of being lookouts and tool carriers, but a few women actually led criminal enterprises which planned and executed large scale jewellery robberies. Margaret Gardiner, for instance, was a forty-two-year-old woman who, in 1907, led a gang of thieves who stole between £15,000 and £20,000 in jewellery, money and securities from a private trunk being loaded onto a train at Manchester's Central Station. The name of the trunk's owner was never revealed publicly, but Margaret Gardiner certainly knew of its presence, and took the simple step of telling railway porters that the trunk was hers, and that she had decided at the last minute not to travel on that day. Instead, Margaret would resume control of the trunk and take it back home. Porters obligingly handed over the item, and Gardiner then disappeared from the station. She was subsequently arrested as she stepped off a train in Liverpool, but by that time much of the jewellery had been pawned, and other items in the trunk had been distributed to Margaret's various accomplices. The theft, and Margaret Gardiner's later trial, was reported in newspapers across Britain. After many months in prison, on remand, she was tried for the crime, found guilty, and sentenced to nine months' imprisonment, with hard labour. Gardiner's crime achieved celebrity status partly because of the scale of the theft (£15,000 in 1907 is probably equivalent to roughly £2,000,000 in 2022) and partly because she was a woman. Female jewel robbers were certainly a considerable rarity in Edwardian England. In reality, though, the majority of the Manchester jewel thieves caught between 1850 and 1950 were also very different from the well-to-do, dapper and daring criminals so liked by newspapers and novelists. Lucky Edgar certainly came from a reasonably affluent background in the Southport area. However, the majority of Manchester's jewel thieves were undoubtedly from working-class origins (often from the poorer areas of Ancoats and Angel Meadow) and saw the theft of expensive items of jewellery as being one clear way of escaping from the daily grind of desperate poverty.

In September 1922, for example, a considerable quantity of gold, diamond and platinum jewels were stolen from the Manchester warehouse of a notable

Front view of Manchester Central Station (now GMEX). (© David Dixon)

A typical Victorian street in Ancoats. (© WythenshaweMike)

local merchant named J. Harold Kippax. The stolen items were valued at between £3,000 and £4,000, and the thieves were traced quite rapidly to a house in Salford. Three young males were arrested by local police – John Dignan, aged seventeen, his younger brother Francis, aged just fourteen, and a seventeen-year-old named William Lewis. The Dignans were reported as living at an address on Halton Street, Salford, while Lewis lived nearby at Phoebe Street. All three boys grew up together along Regent Road in Salford, and came from working-class families where money was perpetually short. Lewis's father was a general warehouseman, and his elder brothers worked as bottle washers and railway carriage cleaners. The Dignan brothers' father, Patrick, worked as a stevedore on the Manchester Ship Canal. John and Francis Dignan, along with William Lewis, all seem to have participated equally in the Kippax warehouse robbery. Despite their youth, the boys were all remanded in custody to await trial at Manchester Assizes, though fourteen-year-old Francis Dignan was allowed to stay at the Denmark Street shelter during his period on remand. The boys had been caught red-handed with Kippax jewels and money, and their downfall had really been assured from the moment an anonymous informant (possibly another family member) had forwarded one of the stolen jewels to the police through the post. Whoever sent the jewel had been unable to afford postage costs, and the police had to pay a one penny surcharge when they accepted the package from the postal authorities. The three teenage boys were hard up, down-at-heel jewel thieves, almost certainly motivated by dire economic necessity. This type of poor local miscreant was probably the most common kind of jewel thief to be found in Manchester during the period between 1850 and 1950.

THE HIGHS AND LOWS OF SNOOZING

During the Victorian era, a rich panoply of slang words arose to describe both crimes, and the people that committed them. A cly faker, for example, was a thief who specialised in stealing handkerchiefs, and a fine wirer was a highly skilled pickpocket. A snoozer, though, was a criminal who focussed exclusively upon stealing from hotels. Snoozers were looked upon as being the aristocrats of the criminal world during much of the nineteenth century. The nickname of 'snoozer' is, however, something of a misnomer, because the last thing on a successful hotel thief's mind was 'snoozing'. The snoozer had to stay awake during the hours of darkness in order to sneak into guests' bedrooms, very often with the guests asleep in their beds and make off quietly with whatever money, jewellery and other items that could be found. The classical snoozer was also something of a charmer, well dressed, and able to converse with people in an amiable fashion, in order to find out which hotel guests were wealthy and which were not. Victorian hotels in Manchester and elsewhere were a perfect place for such thievery because (in an era before fingerprints and hotel detectives) security was often lax, and bedroom door locks were mostly basic and easy to pick. There was also an abundance of ready cash, and other items, to be found in Manchester hotel bedrooms. Guests needed a substantial supply of money, because hotel food and drink tended to be very expensive, and (perhaps surprisingly) the average Victorian hotel guest in Manchester and elsewhere was a very generous tipper – providing tips for a whole range of hotel services. This kind of environment, with large amounts of money circulating between guests and staff, made snoozing a very attractive proposition for a wide range of Victorian ne'er-do-wells. The mid-Victorian period was probably the high point of snoozing in Manchester. During the 1850s, in particular, there were a number of high profile Manchester snoozing cases that were reported avidly in newspapers and journals across the UK. The 1850s, of course, were a time when Britain stood in relative isolation as the world's only superpower, and Manchester was also at the peak of its greatness as the planet's first truly industrialised city. Merchants, traders and crooks from around the world flocked to Manchester's best hotels in order to seize the opportunities on offer in a city where incredible wealth and riches were generated on a very regular basis. The Queen's Hotel on Portland Street, the Albion Hotel at the junction of Oldham Street and Piccadilly, and the Royal Hotel on Mosley Street were particular favourites of the world's affluent money makers, and these elite guests attracted in their wake some of the most daring and ambitious snoozers from France, America and elsewhere.

Above: Queen's Hotel, 1888.

Left: Albion Hotel. (© manchesterhistory.net)

Royal Hotel plaque, erected in 1986. (© Simon Harriyot)

In early February 1854, Frenchman Louis Montagnet checked into the Queen's Hotel. However, he wasn't a resident for long. Within two hours, Montagnet had stolen nearly £10,000 in bills of exchange and other property, from multiple bedrooms, and then headed off to Victoria Station. The robbery was a huge one, equivalent to well over £1,000,000 in modern terms, and the fact that Montagnet could steal so much from a few bedrooms, in so short a time, gives a clear indication of just how much wealth was present in 1850s Manchester. Montagnet, possibly from a merchant background himself, shaved off his moustache and changed his clothes before trying to make his escape on board a train to Preston. The Frenchman's disguise wasn't enough to fool the Manchester police though – the Gallic snoozer was caught red handed on the Preston bound train, with thousands of pounds worth of exchange bills actually secreted on his person. In the end, Montagnet's audacious robbery had proved to be a complete failure. Nevertheless, the vast wealth on display at Manchester's most opulent hotels meant that other international snoozers would inevitably try to succeed where Louis Montagnet had so obviously failed.

American snoozers, and snoozer gangs, were renowned as being expert practitioners in the art of hotel theft. In the mid-1850s, one such American gang, comprising Oscar Kingston, a Philadelphia grocer and provisions dealer,

Continental bill of exchange. (© Federal government of Switzerland)

Daniel Eugene Branch, who described himself as being a New York lawyer, and a Wisconsin merchant named Benjamin Allen Howard cut a swathe through some of Europe's finest hotels, robbing money and valuables wherever they went. Branch was implicated in some massive thefts from the Hotel de la Rue in Paris, and together with Kingston, he was suspected of being involved in between twelve and fourteen hotel robberies at various locations throughout Europe. Ben Howard, together with Kingston, was also involved in robbing guests at the Great Northern Hotel in London. After robbing the Great Northern, Howard travelled to Liverpool to board the RMS *Persia,* which was due to begin one of its regular runs across the Atlantic to America. Kingston and Branch were scheduled to join him after one last great snoozing spree in the mighty industrial metropolis of Manchester. In early April 1856, Kingston booked himself into the Royal Hotel, while Daniel Branch stayed at the Albion Hotel, which was much favoured by American cotton merchants and traders. Both men began robbing hotel bedrooms with considerable gusto. During the early hours of one particular morning, the occupant of Room 21 at the Royal – a commercial traveller named Edwin Edders – was awoken by the sound of someone rummaging through his trousers at the foot of his bed. Edders had, in fact, discovered Kingston actually in the act of stealing £25 from his room. The commercial traveller's cries of alarm forced Kingston to flee from the room. The 6-foot-tall, well-built American ran across the hotel's public landing, dressed in his underwear, and shot back into his own room. Kingston's flight had, however, been witnessed by the Royal's kitchen maid, who recalled that he was wearing a particularly tight fitting flannel vest and drawers. Kingston was quickly arrested by police, in his hotel bedroom, where they found a steel morticing chisel which could be used to prize open doors and strongboxes. In the same room, Manchester police also found a rather ornate pair of pliers: The two ends of these pliers, when pressed together, formed a barrel, which could be used to turn keys in locks, and thereby open doors. Meanwhile, at the Albion Hotel, Daniel Branch had been very active indeed, robbing at least four hotel bedrooms and also stealing a purse full of American and French coins from the hotel's landlord. Unlike his colleague, however, Branch did manage to get away from Manchester. He went to stay at the Adelphi Hotel in Liverpool, prior to boarding the RMS *Persia* for the journey back to America. Unfortunately for Branch, Manchester detectives were able to quickly track him down, and the fugitive American was arrested in his Adelphi bedroom. Police found a heavy American knuckleduster in Branch's possession, along with shirts and other property belonging to a Spanish resident of the Albion Hotel in Manchester. Branch was taken back to Manchester, and eventually stood trial for the theft of the shirts and other property from the Spaniard's room.

Oscar Kingston, despite being arrested for a crime in Manchester, was taken to London to stand trial at the Old Bailey for his plundering of the Great Northern Hotel. Ben Howard, his accomplice at the Great Northern, was arrested on board the RMS *Persia,* and stood trial alongside Kingston in London. Both men were found guilty and sentenced to five years in prison. Back in Manchester, Daniel Branch was found guilty of theft at the Albion, and received the perhaps surprisingly lenient sentence of just one year's imprisonment. Everyone knew

RMS *Persia* in 1855.

Above: Adelphi Hotel, Liverpool, 1896. (© Rijksmuseum)

Below: American brass knuckles, *c.* 1850s. (© Carol Highsmith Collection)

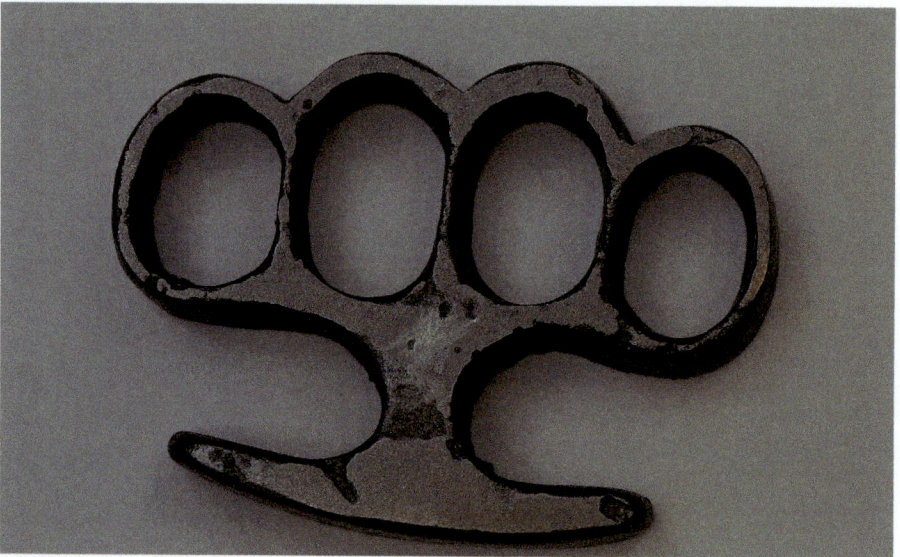

that Branch was something of a master criminal, and a snoozer of the highest calibre, but only the one charge of theft from the Albion's Spanish resident was ever brought against him. The exact reason for this leniency is difficult to explain. However, Daniel Branch (during his time in Manchester) was in possession of diplomatic papers signed by no less a figure than George Dallas, the USA's ambassador to Britain, who had previously been the American Vice-President, under President William Polk. These papers gave Branch diplomatic status as an accredited bearer of dispatches linked to the American legation in Paris. Even in modern times, the question of diplomatic immunity from legal actions remains a thorny issue, but way back in 1856, Daniel Branch's international diplomatic connections may also have encouraged Manchester's judicial authorities to go easy and issue a relatively lenient sentence to the thieving American.

At the time of their capture in Manchester, Branch and Kingston were at the pinnacle of their criminal careers, travelling Europe and stealing money, goods and property from affluent hotel guests. They were elite members of the underworld snoozing fraternity, but Branch in particular still had much in common with many of Manchester's more local and commonplace snoozers.

George Mifflin Dallas, 1792–1864. (© Library of Congress)

While in Manchester, Branch stole shirts belonging to the Albion Hotel's resident Spaniard, Miguel de Buerre, and theft of clothes was one of the most common crimes in Manchester during the entire Victorian period. There was always a market for stolen second-hand clothes, because vast numbers of ordinary Mancunians were simply too poor to buy new items. Indeed, for many Manchester males who enlisted to fight in the First World War, the uniforms issued to them by recruiting sergeants were the first new clothes given to them in their entire lives. Some of the best quality clothing available was purloined by snoozers from Manchester's hotels, and then passed on (via criminal 'fences') to a generally keen and receptive Manchester public. Clothes focussed snoozing seems to have been particularly endemic in 1862. On one particular night in February of that year, a man described as being in his mid-thirties, stout, with dark hair and a black moustache booked into the Royal Hotel. The man carried a black leather bag with him. During the course of the night, the dark-haired man broke into a number of bedrooms, but particularly targetted the possessions of a Mr Lowe, from London. The thief stole Mr Lowe's black overcoat, trousers, pipe, boots, shirts, and several pairs of the unfortunate Londoner's cherished striped socks, before making off into the murky Manchester night. To add insult to injury, the thief left behind him his own boots, which he'd swapped for a pair of Mr Lowe's finest footwear, along with his black leather bag, which was later discovered to contain only a heavy stone, cabbage leaves and firewood. The mysterious thieving hotel guest was never heard from again, and Mr Lowe's garments were never recovered.

Later in the same evening, a similar clothes robbery took place at the Albion Hotel. The perpetrator was dressed in dark clothing, and might possibly have been the same man who'd earlier stolen much of Mr Lowe's wardrobe at the Royal (though on this occasion an eyewitness described the offender as being slender rather than stout). Whoever the offender was, he again escaped into the night, this time with a carpet bag fully laden with stolen clothes, and no one was ever arrested for this particular Albion Hotel robbery. In the same month, of February 1862, a snoozer described as being about thirty years old, with sandy hair and completely bewhiskered, stole a pile of handkerchiefs and shirts, along with a clasp knife, from Manchester's Thatched House Hotel. These snoozer hotel clothes robberies continued right into the late nineteenth century and beyond. In 1891, for example, there were a spate of overcoat thefts from central Manchester hotels, which finally ended when a commercial traveller named John Smith was apprehended at the Queens Hotel, as he attempted to flee from the premises with one of the resident's £50 overcoats.

Manchester hotel robberies, carried out by thieves masquerading as guests, carried on well into the twentieth century. However, by 1900, the heyday of the snoozer was well and truly over. Developments in safes and locking systems presented obvious problems to the criminally inclined, and the greater use of fingerprinting certainly helped police track down snoozers in Manchester and elsewhere. The early 1900s also saw the greater use of hotel detectives in the UK. The phenomenon of the hotel detective, privately employed by hotels to root out thievery in bedrooms and elsewhere, had originated in some of America's most exclusive hotels, such as the Waldorf-Astoria in New York. By September 1901, however, *The Globe* newspaper was able to report that well paid hotel detectives (at least one was being paid the astronomical sum of £1,200 per annum) were making life tough for Britain's snoozers. Hotel thieves were being caught by these house detectives before they could even travel to Manchester. In these circumstances, a repetition of the 1850s, when American snoozers could rob hotels in Paris and London, and then move on to create mayhem in Manchester and Liverpool, was unlikely.

Men's Victorian overcoats, *Gazette of Fashion*, 1872.

Above: Victorian carpet bag, *c.* 1865. (© Metropolitan Museum of Art)

Left: Victorian clasp knife. (© Metropolitan Museum of Art)

STREET CRIME

During the century between 1850 and 1950, virtually every crime imaginable took place on the streets of Manchester, from the 'high' crimes of murder down to the minor offences of begging and 'sleeping out' in doorways and alleys (which was illegal under the terms of the 1824 Vagrancy Act). The multitude of different crimes committed on the streets was reflected in the wide variety of slang phrases used to depict particular types of street criminal. Swell mobsmen, for instance, were usually well-dressed, highly skilled pickpockets who invaded the streets of Manchester on regular occasions in the late nineteenth and early twentieth centuries. In April 1908, for instance, *The Globe* newspaper referred to large numbers of 'swell mobsmen', along with other provincial pickpockets, who were descending on Manchester in order to steal from people who were in the city to witness a crucial local by-election involving the Liberal MP Winston Churchill. This 1908 invasion of Manchester by pickpockets from other parts of the country was by no means unique. In 1895, gangs of London pickpockets were detained in Manchester, and on 16 May 1917, pickpockets from Liverpool, Glasgow and Sheffield flooded into the city to steal from crowds who were cheering on George V and Queen Mary as the royal couple made a whistle-stop wartime tour of Manchester. After they'd arrived in Manchester, one of these wartime pickpocketing gangs concentrated on stealing from the crowds assembled between Whitworth Street and London Road. Another group picked the pockets of people who were watching Queen Mary visit wounded soldiers at the MRI. This group of pickpockets, outside the hospital, were spotted by police officers and pursued in a motor van to Moss Side, where they were eventually arrested. Everyone arrested was found to have previous pickpocketing convictions, and all those found guilty were sentenced to three months in prison.

Less skilled street pickpockets were sometimes referred to as 'gonophs', and in the 1850s at least, Manchester female pickpockets who trained children in the nefarious art of stealing from pockets were often called 'guns'. An experienced Manchester pickpocket might also keep 'picking up' women during this mid-century period, who stole items on behalf of their more experienced criminal boss. The role of women in picking Manchester pockets cannot be overestimated. Particularly in the mid-Victorian period, the height of male fashion was for tight trousers with front pockets, which obviously made unobtrusive pocket-picking quite a challenge (voluminous male overcoats were less of a challenge). By contrast, expansive female bell-shaped crinoline skirts presented the dexterous pickpocket with ample opportunities for theft. These skirts often had pockets on the right side, positioned just under a flounce, which could be picked with

Status: Point in time view as at 05/05/2011.
Changes to legislation: Vagrancy Act 1824 is up to date with all changes known to be in force on or before
04 August 2017. There are changes that may be brought into force at a future date. Changes that have
been made appear in the content and are referenced with annotations. (See end of Document for details)

Vagrancy Act 1824

1824 CHAPTER 83 5 Geo 4

An Act for the Punishment of idle and disorderly Persons, and Rogues and Vagabonds, in England

---

Annotations:

Modifications etc. (not altering text)
C1   Short title given by Short Titles Act 1896 (c. 14)
C2   Preamble omitted under authority of Statute Law Revision Act 1890 (c. 33)

1, 2.   . . . . **F1**

Annotations:

Amendments (Textual)
F1   Ss. 1, 2 repealed by Statute Law Revision Act 1873 (c. 91)

---

3   **Persons committing certain offences how to be punished.**

. . . . **F2**[**F3**every petty chapman or pedlar wandering abroad, and trading without being duly licensed, or otherwise authorized by law; every common prostitute wandering in the public streets or public highways, or in any place of public resort, and behaving in a riotous or indecent manner; and] every person wandering abroad, or placing himself or herself in any public place, street, highway, court, or passage, to beg or gather alms, or causing or procuring or encouraging any child or children so to do; shall be deemed an idle and disorderly person within the true intent and meaning of this Act; and [**F4**, subject to section 70 of the Criminal Justice Act 1982,] it shall be lawful for any justice of the peace to commit such offender (being thereof convicted before him by his own view, or by the confession of such offender, or by the evidence on oath of one or more credible witness or witnesses,) to the house of correction, . . . **F5** for any time not exceeding one calendar month.

1824 Vagrancy Act. (© legislation.gov.uk)

King George V and Queen Mary in 1914. (© Library of Congress)

Modern Whitworth Street. (© Duncan Watts)

some ease by a competent pickpocket, and the pickpocket who created less suspicion when moving close to a particular female target was, of course, another woman. Whole families, including parents and children, could be involved in pickpocketing. In September 1850, the *Hull Packet* newspaper ran a detailed account of the life of a seventeen-year-old Stockport-born pickpocket called Ellen O'Neill. At this time, Ellen was languishing in a Preston gaol, along with her husband and father, awaiting transportation for various pickpocketing offences. Ellen had previously lived in Manchester with her father and husband, and she'd been trained as a pickpocket since the age of fifteen. Moreover, the person that had supervised her training in the art of picking pockets was none other than her elder brother, John, who was so skilful that he could apparently pick a woman's skirt pocket as she was running along a street. Ellen herself proved to be very skilled at pickpocketing, having been taught by her husband how to raise ladies' dresses and steal whatever was present in more intimate underwear pockets.

LE FOLLET
Boules au St. Martin, 69.
Costumes de Humann, r. N.^{le} des petits Champs, 83
Parfumeries de la Société hygiénique, r. J.J. Rousseau, 5.
8, Argyll Place, Regent Street, Londres.

Fashionable tight trousers for men, c. 1853. (© Rijksmuseum)

Female fashions for March 1850. (© Rijksmuseum)

For a time, teenage Ellen had lived with her father in Manchester, and each day, for about six months, she travelled out of Manchester by train, stealing from pockets as she travelled. Her most successful day was when she travelled by train for the short distance between Manchester and Stockport, when she stole £22 from either people on the train, or those in the vicinity of the railway stations. Ellen had worked as a piecer in a Manchester cotton mill since the age of ten, and she had female friends who'd worked in the same mill, and then gravitated to pickpocketing handkerchiefs in the streets, and stealing boots. Victorian handkerchief thieves were sometimes called stock buzzers, and Ellen claimed that her friends were given time off in the afternoons by their male factory overseers in order to go stock buzzing. The proceeds of the girls' thefts (so Ellen alleged) were then shared with their male job superiors.

Ladies' silk handkerchief, *c.* 1850. (© Auckland War Memorial Museum)

Multi-panelled man's handkerchief, *c.* 1850. (© Cooper Hewitt Smithsonian Design Museum)

Other female mill piecers known to Ellen O'Neill supplemented their meagre wages by dollymopping on Oldham Street (i.e. acting as part-time prostitutes). Prostitution at this time was largely tolerated by the police authorities, despite being considered an offence under the terms of various Vagrancy Acts. This tolerant police attitude continued, by and large, throughout the nineteenth century, regardless of the legal measures passed by Parliament. In fact, a Victorian or Edwardian prostitute based in Manchester was far more likely to appear in court for being drunk and disorderly than she was for offering sex on a commercial basis. All this was despite the fact that there were a large number of brothels in Manchester: during the entire Victorian period, there were probably never less than forty brothels in Deansgate alone, and there were twenty or more in Salford. Most of the institutions perceived as being brothels by the police were, in reality, just lodging houses where compliant owners allowed women to bring their clients. Properly enclosed brothels, run by often astute and competent madams, were actually quite rare. Dollymops and full-time prostitutes were a highly visible feature of Manchester street life during this period, both during the daytime and at night. Particular types of dollymop (along with full-time prostitutes) were sometimes associated with particular areas of Manchester. The area just behind Piccadilly, for example, was renowned for the numbers of more mature, sometimes disease-ridden prostitutes that frequented its streets looking for business.

If dollymops and the other 'ladies of the night' were a key, visible feature of Manchester street life, then homeless vagrants and beggars were perhaps an even more distinctive feature of street life and street crime during the period between 1850 and 1950. To be homeless, without sufficient funds to at least rent a room for the night, was an offence under the terms of the Vagrancy Act, which was prosecutable well into the twenty-first century. Those caught 'sleeping out' in

Prostitution etching by Paul-Albert Besnard, *c.* 1886. (© National Gallery of Art)

Royal Infirmary and Piccadilly, Manchester.

6-1-05.

D.R.

Piccadilly and the MRI, *c.* 1905.

alleyways, on benches, and in deserted buildings were prosecuted with intermittent vigour during both the Victorian and Edwardian eras. Police would often wait to sweep an area before enforcing the sleeping out edicts of the Vagrancy legislation. As a consequence, large numbers of alleged vagrants could appear in police court docks at the same time. Sometimes, the offenders were treated with sympathy and understanding, and on other occasions they were not. On 8 December 1903, twenty-nine men appeared together, in an overcrowded Manchester Police Court dock, after being arrested for 'sleeping out'. An obviously sympathetic magistrate commented that far more should be done to help such individuals. After a day on the streets, a night spent in a deserted brickworks was a popular recourse for many unfortunate Manchester vagrants. During one night in February 1902, twenty police officers arrested forty such unfortunates for sleeping out at a brickworks. Those with no previous vagrancy convictions were sent to prison for a day, and those with a history of vagrancy received sentences of between seven days and one month in prison. The impact of these arrests was minimal because a year later, in February 1903, dozens of individuals were still being detained and sent to prison for sleeping out in north Manchester brickwork drying sheds and brickcrofts. Although begging as a whole was an offence, it was professional beggars – those who earned a reasonable or good living from begging in the streets – who aroused the particular hostility of many ordinary Mancunians. In summer 1921, for instance, an elderly man called John Belford was arrested for begging. Belford was dressed in rags, and appeared to be in a pitiable condition.

THE BEGGAR'S PETITION.

Beggars' petition from the *London Serio Journal*, 1872.

However, by the time he appeared in court, during early July, it was discovered that Belford had £150 in a Post Office savings account and possessed stocks and shares worth in excess of £1,000. The magistrate sent Belford to prison for two weeks, and ordered that the rather affluent beggar paid for his own food and keep during his time behind bars. Belford's case was an extreme one, but there were other professional beggars who made a reasonably good living on the streets of Manchester. At the height of the First World War, on 30 August 1917, a seventeen-year-old male from Wigan called John Strong was sent to prison for a month for begging in Manchester. John came into the city on two occasions each week in order to beg on the streets, and usually made £5 a day when he did so – quite a sizable sum in 1917, roughly equivalent to about £370 a day in 2022.

Not all begging cases that came to court in Manchester led to convictions. In summer 1878, for example, two nuns from the Sisters of Mercy Order, founded by Catherine McAuley in 1831, appeared in court on vagrancy charges. The Sisters of Mercy were known as the 'walking nuns', who actively engaged with their local communities, and went out seeking alms to help with their care of the Manchester elderly and infirm. Unfortunately, two nuns from the order made the mistake of

Statue of Catherine McAuley, founder of the Sisters of Mercy. (© Spleodrach)

walking from their Manchester convent to the house of William Raynor Wood in Prestwich in order to seek his help with their charitable endeavours. Raynor Wood was a prominent local Justice of the Peace (JP) and a successful merchant, who lived in Prestwich with his wife Isobel and two small children. The nuns might have expected a sympathetic hearing from Raynor Wood, but the JP swiftly had both women detained in his servants' hall, for begging, and called the police. The two nuns, clad in their Order's habits, spent the night in the local police station (though not in the cells) before appearing in court on the following morning, charged with contravening vagrancy legislation. An astonished magistrate quickly dismissed all charges, and Raynor Wood was made to look rather foolish. The Chancellor of the Duchy of Lancaster speedily wrote a letter to Raynor Wood criticising his actions, and warning that any further 'mistakes' would lead to his removal from the county's list of available JPs.

THE SCUTTLERS

During the last three decades of the nineteenth century, the nature of street crime in Manchester was changed considerably by the advent of the scuttler gangs. These gangs of young people, predominantly made up of males and females aged between fourteen and eighteen (though gang leaders could be in their early twenties), dominated many of the streets in Manchester's poorer neighbourhoods. Working-class scuttler youths fought each other on the streets in considerable numbers – *The Gorton Reporter,* for example, revealed that 500 scuttlers, from two rival gangs, had clashed on one particular occasion during 1879. Scuttler crimes were mostly ones of physical violence. Gang members assaulted scuttlers from rival groups with considerable venom, causing serious injuries and a few deaths. The motivation behind the formation of scuttler gangs is difficult to determine with precision. Male gang members were mostly in poorly paid employment, with little hope of progression, and gang membership certainly provided opportunities for 'letting off steam'. Scuttler counter-culture offered prestige to those who could exhibit machismo and toughness by beating up rival scuttlers and police officers. Scuttlers who were sent to prison for repeat offences might also be cheered from the public galleries (by fellow scuttlers) as they made their way out of the courtroom to begin yet another term of imprisonment. The testosterone-fuelled, violent youth culture of the scuttlers was mirrored in other British cities – Birmingham, for instance, had its violent slogger gangs, which later metamorphosed into the more criminally minded (and famous) Peaky Blinders. In an era when a Manchester scuttler or a Birmingham slogger had little spare money to engage in other activities, gang membership offered an alternative, violent way of life, which provided some bonds of loyalty, companionship, and even possible avenues for advancement. The streets where scuttlers grew up became the focus of intense loyalty, and gangs were named after these streets. Thus, there were the Bengal Tigers, who hailed from Bengal Street, the Meadow Lads from Angel Meadow, the Lime Street Boys, and the Greengate gang from

Salford. During the early 1890s, the Greengate scuttlers were led by a tough 5 feet 4 inch tall labourer called William Henry Brooke, who was in his early twenties. Brooke was in and out of Strangeways prison on repeated occasions, thereby earning himself considerable status amongst fellow scuttlers, and in 1894 he was arrested for stealing a shawl (probably for a scuttler girlfriend) from a Rochdale washing line.

Scuttlerism also provided its male and female adherents with a distinct visual identity. Many decades before distinctive clothes marked out Mods, Rockers, Teddy Boys and Punks, scuttlers were dressing themselves in a very different way to the average Victorian youth. The Manchester male scuttler donned bell bottomed trousers, brass tipped clogs, and brightly coloured neckerchiefs. He also had a very distinctive haircut, involving a shaved back and sides, with the hair on the top left-hand side of the head being left to grow so that it could be plastered down over the left eye. Ideally, this 'donkey fringe' still had to be visible when the scuttler donned a jauntily angled peaked cap. Female scuttlers also had

Bengal Street, once home of the Bengal Tigers scuttler gang. (© Clem Rutter)

Inset: Scuttler William Brooke of the Greengate gang, 1890.

Victorian linen shawl, *c.* 1870–80. (© Auckland War Memorial Museum)

their own distinctive dress style, involving the wearing of a shawl and a vertically striped skirt. Suitably clad, these female scuttlers could then join their male colleagues in pitched battles on Manchester streets, intimidate possible witnesses to fights, or lure rival male gang members into ambushes. Belts with brass buckles (wrapped tightly around the hands) were a favoured scuttler weapon, along with stones wrapped in handkerchiefs, which were then hurled like a biblical sling. Knives were also used, sometimes with fatal consequences, in scuttler street fights. On 16 December 1894, scuttlers attacked a collier named John Wilcock, on Deansgate, with belts, bats and knives. Wilcock was stabbed in the back by two scuttlers, named Thomas Darlington and John Elliot. The collier survived the brutal attack, and Darlington and Elliot were subsequently sentenced to prison terms of three years and five years respectively, for feloniously wounding Wilcock. Two years prior to the attack on John Wilcock, sixteen-year-old scuttler William Willan, of the Bradford Street gang, had been found guilty of the murder of Peter Kennedy, a member of the rival Lime Street Boys scuttler gang. William and two other Bradford Street scuttlers had cornered Kennedy on the corner of Great Ancoats Street. It was Willan, however, who had delivered the fatal knife

Bradford Street, once home of the Bradford Street Boys. (© Humphrey Bolton)

wound to Kennedy. Willan was sentenced to hang, but his youth, together with a huge petition for clemency signed by 25,000 people, and a letter asking for mercy from the Manchester detective Jerome Caminada, was enough for the convicted murderer to be granted a commutation. Willan spent eight years in prison before being released from custody. The former scuttler, who began courting Caminada's daughter, Florence May, after his release, proved to be a thoroughly reformed character. He worked as a cooper, married Florence May, and became the proprietor of a thriving fish and chip shop.

William Willan's release from custody, and the beginning of his new reformed life, coincided roughly with the decline and eclipse of the scuttler phenomenon. By 1900, youths from Salford, Gorton, Openshaw and the other poorer parts of Manchester were being enticed into joining other less violent activities at burgeoning boys' clubs, such as the Salford Lads Club. Association football was also growing in popularity with working-class boys across the city, and during the early decades of the twentieth century, the lure of cinemas – showing silent films and then talkies – was increasingly being felt. Working-class youths had attractions and opportunities that didn't involve mass brawls and battles on the streets. As a result, the era of the scuttler gangs drew gradually to a close.

Salford Lads Club. (© Repton1x)

BIBLIOGRAPHY

Buckley, A., *Bob Horridge's Remarkable Career of Crime*, victorian-supersleuth.com [accessed 17.11.2021].

Carsten, F. L., *The Rise of Fascism* (Methuen, 1978).

Chesney, K., *The Victorian Underworld* (Readers Union, 1970).

Coates, K. (ed.), *Tom Mann's Memoirs* (Spokesman, 2008).

O'Neill, J., *Crime City: Manchester's Victorian Underworld* (Milo Books, 2008).

Onyourdoorstepmcr.co.uk/scuttler-gangs [accessed 15.05.2022].

Smith, H. L., *The British Women's Suffrage Campaign 1866–1928* (Routledge, 2010).

The Story of the Scuttlers, manchestereveningnews.co.uk [accessed 20.02.2009].

Walters, M., *Feminism: A Very Short Introduction* (OUP, 2005).

www.britishnewspaperarchive.co.uk

www.in2013dollars.com (UK inflation calculator)

ACKNOWLEDGEMENTS

The authors would like to express their particular thanks to David Boardman at manchesterhistory.net and to Pamela Lynch of Davenham. In addition, the authors would like to express their gratitude to the many libraries, archives, museums and private photographers who have allowed us access to their varied collections. Every effort has been made to fulfil requirements with regards to copyright matters. The authors and publisher will be glad to rectify any omissions at the earliest opportunity.

ABOUT THE AUTHORS

Adrian's family links to Manchester go back at least 180 years. In the early 1840s, his great-great-grandfather (born in Spain) travelled to Manchester, married an Irish girl, and spent the next forty years working as a cotton packer and carder in the city's cotton mills. Adrian himself spent much of his youth in Whalley Range and East Didsbury, attended Manchester University as both an undergraduate and a postgraduate, and then trained as a teacher in various Manchester schools. He also worked in the city's FE sector for nine years, and became involved in trade union education at Salford Quays. Dawn, born and raised in Stoke, shares Adrian's enthusiasm for all aspects of Manchester's history. She is a graduate of Staffordshire University, and has written extensively on Manchester's immense and varied suffragette past.

Also by the same authors:
A–Z of Northwich & Around: People, Places, History (Amberley Publishing, 2019)
Northwich & Around in 50 Buildings (Amberley Publishing, 2021)
Chester's Military Heritage (Amberley Publishing, 2021)
Secret Northwich & Around (Amberley Publishing, 2022)
Staffordshire's Military Heritage (Amberley Publishing, 2022)